PRAISE FOR BETRAYED BY WORK

"This groundbreaking book validates the experiences, and damage done, from being fired while living in a culture in which so much of our worth comes from 'what we do' and 'where we work.' *Betrayed by Work* has informed and inspired me about how to better protect myself as an employee, as well as how to be a more attuned, humanistic supervisor."

—**Gina DelJones**, LSW, clinical research manager at The Center for Great Expectations

"*Betrayed by Work* lends humanity to the oft overlooked reality of women's experiences and struggles in the workplace. It is truly an essential read and valuable toolkit for anyone at any stage of their career."

—**Kate Speir**, senior vice president at Itinera Infrastructure & Concessions

"*Betrayed by Work* addresses a wide gap in our understanding of human and emotional values in the workplace and shows us how women have personally experienced being mistreated and undervalued. Their stories are moving and inspiring. Having been 'on both sides of the desk' in the process described in the book, I know that it often could have and should have been handled much differently.

Now we have some urgently needed solutions. Kudos to the authors for sharing these powerful stories and insights!"

—**G. Gregory Tobin,** former general manager of A.A. World Services and author of The Good Pope

"Losing my job was one of the most lonely and isolating experiences I ever went through, and this book would have been a bright light during a very dark time. This book would have made me feel understood and not so alone. It would have brought me solace. For anyone who has ever experienced the trauma of being torn from your livelihood and workday community, this book is for you."

—**Wendy Jessica,** job loss survivor

"What we do for work identifies us and becomes the mission/vision/purpose and calling in our lives. This is the first book that I know of that truly helps you learn from women from many professional sectors how to recover from big setbacks in our work lives. It's a must read.

—**Dr. Elena Pezzini,** organizational psychologist

"Emerging science proves our choices and decisions—including our engagement, commitment, and loyalty at work—are more often driven by feelings and emotions than by our minds. *Betrayed by Work* showcases the harm done when leaders ignore this truth. This important book contributes an essential voice to the ever growing call for more caring, supportive, and humane leadership."

—**Mark C. Crowley,** author of *Lead From the Heart: Transformational Leadership for the 21st Century*

"*Betrayed by Work* is a long overdue text that provides a conduit for expression, validation, and healing from the life-altering experience of being fired. This book is a must-read that gives a deep and personal look into the experience of women at work, offering practical guidance at a crucial time. The potential for growth and change here is enormous, not only for employees, but also employers and HR [professionals] around the globe. *Betrayed by Work* could be the new 'How To' handbook on humanizing downsizing, layoffs, and firings to mitigate the damage done to confidence and reputation on both sides."

—**Cameron Hartl**, executive coach and job loss survivor

"You're not the only one! As a management consultant and coach, I hear many stories of women feeling defeated and deflated—before, during, and after a termination experience. This book boldly asserts what often goes unsaid—that you are still whole, still deserving, still worthy. The authors courageously advance this hope-filled narrative: termination is just a moment—what have you learned? What's next?"

—**Tracey K. Allard**, strategy, culture, & race equity consultant

BETRAYED

EXIT

BY WORK

BETRAYED BY WORK

Women's Stories of Trauma, Healing and Hope after Being Fired

**JULIA ERICKSON, MBA,
AND SUZANNE VOSBURG, PHD**

CORAL GABLES

For permission requests, please contact the publisher at:

Mango Publishing Group
2850 Douglas Road, 2nd Floor
Coral Gables, FL 33134 USA
info@mango.bz

For special orders, quantity sales, course adoptions and corporate sales, please email the publisher at sales@mango.bz. For trade and wholesale sales, please contact Ingram Publisher Services at customer.service@ingramcontent.com or +1.800.509.4887.

Betrayed By Work: Women's Stories of Trauma, Healing, and Hope After Being Fired

ISBN: (p) 978-1-64250-564-1 (e) 978-1-64250-565-8

LCCN: Pending

BISAC: BUS109000, BUSINESS & ECONOMICS / Women in Business

This is a work describing personal experiences of the author. Therefore, some names and details may have been altered in order to protect the privacy of individuals. Further, this book is not intended as a substitute for the advice of a trained medical professional. The reader should regularly consult a physician in matters relating to his/her mental health and particularly with respect to any symptoms that may require diagnosis or medical attention.

To the women in these pages,

who didn't see it coming,

who did and survived,

and all the women who will ultimately transcend.

TABLE OF CONTENTS

FOREWORD

When my dad, Ernie Thompson, was a teenager, he had a
job at a bowling alley, setting pins. The conditions and the
pay were terrible, so he organized his fellow pinsetters
to demand more for their labor. The boss looked at the
young people and said to them, "Ernie here appears to be
dissatisfied. Are any of the rest of you dissatisfied?" Face-
to-face with their employer, they all retreated. The boss
turned to my dad and said the inevitable, "Well, Ernie, since
you don't like it here, you don't have to work here anymore."
Ernie would go on to be a leader of the union movement, with
many big wins to his name, but he never forgot that episode
in the bowling alley.

Julia Erickson and Suzanne Vosburg, in their timely book
Betrayed by Work, open the story up for me. My dad always
related that episode as teaching him something about
organizing—what it took to get people ready to stand up to
the boss. Reading *Betrayed by Work*, I can imagine him as an
eager young man batted off by a powerful opponent and left
with the embarrassment, chagrin, and fear that seared the
memory into his consciousness.

It is this searing into consciousness that concerns Suzanne
and Julia: that getting fired is not a trivial event, healed by
a few platitudes, but a deeper shock to our sense of self,
our *amour-propre*, as French philosopher Jean-Jacques
Rousseau put it—the sense that we are worthy because our
goodness is reflected back to us by others. When, instead,

the mirror suggests that we are worthless, the *amour-propre* is tarnished and not easily repaired.

Julia and Suzanne take us inside the "what happened" of getting fired—getting called into an office or asked to attend a Zoom meeting; getting some kind of message of dismissal; being asked to leave, perhaps without even a chance to collect one's belongings or say goodbye. The minutiae of these events—I was just back from sick leave; I couldn't get my things; no one would look at me—takes us inside the injurious process and leaves us gasping along with the storyteller.

In the course of my career as a psychiatrist, I've watched two trends. On the one hand, acknowledgement of the toxicity of trauma has broken through all efforts to suppress it. Not only in psychiatry, but also in society, we have come to understand the vast psychic harms that follow disasters, wars, and all kinds of individual injury from rape to car accidents. Many facets of society have become "trauma-informed," giving us a new and useful language for helping people through the hurts that linger in the aftermath of terrifying and life-threatening events. This book adds toxic layoffs to the list of events that can have this stunning effect on our lives and our brains.

On the other hand, I've also watched the undermining of society, the stripping of shared resources of all kinds—from defunding unemployment offices to eliminating public health workers. This has been carried out under the ideology referred to as "neoliberalism," which was explained by British Prime Minister Margaret Thatcher, when she said there was no such thing as society, only individuals. What she and President Ronald Regan and other proponents of neoliberalism really meant was, "You have to break some eggs to make an omelet, so I'm going to break your eggs and I'll have an omelet." If you're not clear how the celebration of individualism actually means transferring wealth to the already rich, you are not alone. What I'm sure is clear is that there is such a thing as society and people need to be able to find a well-funded, well-staffed unemployment office when they've just been thrown out of a job.

That was not what we had in January 2020 when the new coronavirus, SARS-CoV-2, hit. The only tools at the disposal of public health were those time-tested interventions of quarantine and social distancing. Governments ordered that we shelter in place; workplaces emptied as a result. By August 2020, 29.2 million people had filed for unemployment benefits, scrambling to get through poorly supported phone lines, crashing outdated computer systems, and enduring waits of weeks or months before checks started to arrive. For a brief period, the government provided generous disaster relief but then the ideology of "my omelet" kicked in, and support was withdrawn, leaving people gasping in uncertainty and terror.

In my studies of what makes a society and its people healthy, it's definitely not the "my omelet" philosophy we've been living under for forty years. Rather, we prosper from meeting the basic needs of everyone, among them a chance to see our own goodness reflected by the places in which we work. It is at moments of transition that the nature of our collective is revealed. A callous firing, a world without a safety net—these are more than harms to the self; they are symptoms of the collapse of our togetherness.

Suzanne and Julia bravely call for a different kind of world, one in which we think and act from our solidarity, one in which we build workplaces to mirror to people that they are good and kind and worthy of dignified treatment. Their lists of advice call us to a breakfast table brimming with food for all, joy for all, kindness for all. This is the kind of world in which we will prosper now and, in that security, turn our attention to the haunting backlog of problems that hover over our future: climate change, ecological devastation, inequality, and more. It may seem overly simplistic to say it begins with respect for the worker who is to be let go. I think it is not: each step towards justice, kindness, and respect for the worker's *amour-propre* is a step in the direction of a healthy and competent society.

Mindy Thompson Fullilove, MD
February 14, 2021

PREFACE

We began writing this book about women's unexpected job loss and its impact before 2020. Before the COVID-19 pandemic and the economic disaster that followed. Before George Floyd's murder and the ensuing racial reckoning. Before a Black and South Asian woman Vice President was elected after one of the most acrimonious elections in modern times—her gender and her race both being firsts.

The events of 2020 amplified the messages already in our book: repeating themes of gender bias, structural and personal racism, and a dysfunctional workplace culture that dehumanizes people in the job termination process. We explore these ideas in Chapter 30 through our lens of women's experiences—women of all races and ethnicities, ages and professions.

Job loss is not gender-specific, and we hope this book will also help men find their way through their job losses to healing. Our focus is on women because we're women and know many women who have lost their jobs in one way or another.

During the Covid-19 pandemic, tens of millions of jobs disappeared seemingly overnight. Between mid-March and August 2020, 57.4 million Americans filed for unemployment,[12] Although women held down most essential jobs that still existed outside of the home during COVID-19[3], we were startled to find Bureau of Labor Statistics[4] data revealing that women also bore a significant amount of COVID-19 job loss. In fact, the *New York Times* used the term "Shecession"[5] to emphasize the degree to which jobs lost during the COVID-19 shutdown were lost by women.[6]

Data from October 2020 showed that 80 percent of jobs lost in September 2020 were lost by women, one-third by Latinas.[7] When employment dropped sharply in the COVID-19 labor market, Black women faced the largest losses.[8]

1   Jack Kelly, "Jobless Claims: 574 Million Americans Have Sought Unemployment Benefits Since Mid-March…," *Forbes*, 8/20/2020 www.forbes.com/sites/jackkelly/2020/08/20/jobless-claims-574-million-americans-have-sought-unemployment-benefits-since-mid-marchover-1-million-people-filed-last-week/#39f831016d59.

2   Tony Romm, Jeff Stein & Erica Werner, "2.4 Million Americans Filed Jobless Claims Last Week…," *The Washington Post*, 5/21/2020, www.washingtonpost.com/business/2020/05/21/unemployment-claims-coronavirus.

3   Campbell Robertson & Robert Gebelof, "How Millions of Women Became the Most Essential Workers in America," The New York Times, 4/18/2020 www.nytimes.com/2020/04/18/us/coronavirus-women-essential-workers.html; Alisha Haridasani Gupta, "Why Did Hundreds of Thousands of Women Drop Out of the Work Force?" *The New York Times*, 10/3/2020 www.nytimes.com/2020/10/03/us/jobs-women-dropping-out-workforce-wage-gap-gender.html.

4   Eleni Karageorge," COVID-19 recession is tougher on women," US Bureau of Labor Statistics Monthly Labor Review, September 2020 www.bls.gov/opub/mlr/2020/beyond-bls/covid-19-recession-is-tougher-on-women.htm.

5   For ease of writing & communication, we use the pronouns she / her.

6   Alisha Haridasani Gupta, "Why Some Women Call This a 'Shecession,'" *The New York Times*, 5/9/2020 www.nytimes.com/2020/05/09/us/unemployment-coronavirus-women.html.

7   Avie Schneider, Andrea Hsu & Scott Horsely, "Multiple Demands Causing Women to Abandon Workforce," *NPR*, 10/2/2020 www.npr.org/sections/coronavirus-live-updates/2020/10/02/919517914/enough-already-multiple-demands-causing-women-to-abandon-workforce.

8   Elise Gould & Valerie Gould, "Black workers face two of the most lethal preexisting conditions for coronavirus—racism and economic inequality," Economic Policy Institute, 6/1/2020 www.epi.org/publication/black-workers-covid.

Considering this sudden, macro-level job loss, we wondered if our book still mattered. Were women still being betrayed by work by being let go from their jobs in ways that were traumatic? Did we still think that there could be a more compassionate way of separating women from their work?

The answer to both questions is an unqualified *yes*.

Women's experiences of losing their jobs and the emotional damage caused by this trauma remained the same during the pandemic. BIPOC (Black, Indigenous and People of Color) women have experienced employment bias and structural racism for hundreds of years.

The methods by which women were let go were as brutal and broken as they were before COVID-19. A ten-minute Zoom call, a text message, an email. "Your last day is today." No advance notice. For too many, little or no severance. Social media revealed that women who lost their jobs during COVID-19 felt as betrayed and traumatized as the women in our book. They had similar feelings of abandonment, lost identity, loneliness, anger and, yes, betrayal from broken promises.

Being unexpectedly let go initiates a traumatic cascade of events for which there is no easy off-ramp.

We also began writing this book before George Floyd was murdered in Minneapolis by a white police officer and protests against systemic anti-Black police practices as well as white supremacist structures erupted across the US and the world. Examining and eliminating structural racism is now a stated focus for many corporations.

The stories in this book told by Black women and women of color clearly reveal the insidious structural racism in several industries. While they are individual stories, they show patterns of the same dominant structures being protested: structures and practices that exist to enable white people—predominantly men, but white women as well—to maintain power and position in the workplace. Will new awareness shift these inequalities and begin to eliminate structural racism? We hope so.

It is with hope for both of these structural challenges that we offer *Betrayed by Work* as a starting point.

Julia Erickson[9] and Suzanne Vosburg, January 2021

---

9 **Conflict of Interest Statement:** Julia is an executive coach and some of her clients' stories appear in this collection. Other storytellers found their own coaches or therapists. Even so, this book is not intended to be an "infomercial" for Julia's services or for coaching. We hope readers will take away the point that you don't have to travel the road back from being fired alone.

Introduction

I'M WHAT?!!

Imagine you're a professional, mid-career woman and you get fired. After the "I'm what??!!" reaction, what do you do?

This *cri de coeur* (cry from the heart) is both emotional and practical; it is especially felt by professional women who expect, and are expected, to move forward continually in their careers. How do you cope with feeling victimized (or being victimized) by people for whom you worked, and sometimes even by the operational structures of today's workplace?

Existing books on getting fired offer suggestions that emphasize getting on with it.

But what if you can't just "get on with it?"

Getting fired is one of life's most difficult emotional experiences. Selfhood is taken away in an instant. We experience a sudden powerlessness that destroys our confidence and feelings of self-worth. We grieve. We feel broken. It affects our self-esteem. We feel betrayed. It is traumatic, isolating, and, in fact, devastating. And that's just on the inside!

Losing your job affects your financial well-being. It determines how many more mortgage payments, tuition payments, car payments, or credit card payments you can make until you have to come up with other plans.

(Refinance? Take your kid out of college? Lose the car? Skip some credit card payments?) It affects your professional identity and your ability to look for other work. It shocks us back from what we thought was true and makes us wonder what was real and what was not. *Job loss affects our entire life.* And even though the financial piece of this equation is all-encompassing, for many women, the internal piece—the emotional experience—has even more salience and consequence.

How, then, does a woman navigate the emotional impact of this event?

With other women.

If you've found this book after getting downsized, laid off, or fired, come join us and meet kindred spirits here. This is how we found each other and decided to write this book. When we needed to heal after our own job losses (jobs we lost even though we excelled at them), it helped when women came forward of their own accord and told us, *I had the same thing happen to me and this is what I did.* Sharing our stories and listening to other women's stories helped us feel better. Listening to other voices helped us hear our own voices more clearly. Through the sharing of these experiences came the rich connectedness we and other women needed to make meaning out of this traumatic experience and move into the next phase of our lives with greater self-confidence, agency, and fulfillment. These conversations became the impetus for this book.

Many of the women who tell us their stories in these pages were let go from their jobs without any warning, without any obvious reason, or without any opportunity to prepare for such a devastating, life-altering loss. None engaged in aberrant behaviors. All were committed to doing a good job. All were competent. Most were in the middle of their career lives. Asking themselves what had happened was an effort to regain some semblance of personal power, but, for most of us there was no clear answer to that question, because we hadn't done anything that warranted losing our jobs, our livelihoods, and our ways of life, and we certainly had not done anything to warrant the way we were treated.

With few exceptions, the way employers delivered the news compounded the hurt. Curt at best, mean at worst, the manner of dismissal felt angry and hostile. Some women's last experience of their workplace (after years of working there) was immediately being accompanied out by a security guard after being asked to retrieve their belongings. They couldn't even say goodbye. Others were called at home on maternity leave and told they were no longer needed, so they should come pick up their things. And now, in this time of COVID-19, some were let go on Zoom calls.

The experience of being unexpectedly dismissed from our work without any further discussion indelibly imprinted our lives. We women felt completely betrayed by our employers. We were betrayed by work.

Betrayed. It's a big word. Its meanings include to deliver or expose an enemy by treachery or disloyalty; to disappoint the hopes or expectations of; be disloyal to; isolation of a person's trust or confidence; and violation of a moral standard.

For the women in this book, *betrayed* was the only word big enough to encompass the experience. Up until the time we got fired, we trusted our bosses and expected our employers to act honorably. We thought they appreciated our work and our contributions. Many of us had no sense that something like this could happen to us; people just didn't *do* things like this. We worked with these people. We liked these people. We thought they liked us. We *leaned in*. And suddenly, we learned they had been plotting behind our backs to get rid of us. That knowledge shook us to our very core.

Many women have struggled through this betrayal with little validation or support. In our search for resources to help our friends and colleagues, we found few books that contemplated the emotional experience of unexpected job loss. We found academic work,[10] but most people don't have access to papers from research databases. Most books move quickly past the actual job loss and fast-forward to the "how-tos" or the "right steps" of searching for a job. We loved the constructive suggestions.

However, when the women we talked to were first let go, they couldn't immediately take practical steps to look for new work because they felt too traumatized and vulnerable from the experience of losing their jobs. None of us could keep moving forward in a linear fashion. We needed something more emotionally intelligent than a "Dust yourself off" or "Suck it up, Buttercup" approach. Specifically, by asking women to tell their stories about losing their jobs

---

10   Gowan MA (2014), Moving from job loss to career management: The past, present, and future of involuntary job loss research. Human Resource Management Review, 24, 258–270; Gowan and Gatewood (1997), A model of response to the stress of involuntary job loss. Human Resource Management Review, 7, 277–297.

unexpectedly and their journeys afterward, we begin to identify an interval between getting fired and being able to confidently, and even enthusiastically, apply for new work.

This emotional span needs attention.

These stories offer the kind of support women wish they had had to get through the difficult time immediately following being fired or laid off. We hope there is even more attention to be found, perhaps by you who are looking in the "professional women," "self-help," "women's interest," "HR," or other bookshelves. By paying attention, we hope to provide a realistic framework for processing the emotional experience of job loss by sharing firsthand experiences of women from a variety of professions.

To do so, we collected stories of how women were betrayed by work. We capture the "I'm what??!!" reaction to the shock of being fired, and share how women handled themselves, their loved ones, and the many complicated facets of their lives in the process of figuring out what to do next, all the while feeling betrayed and untethered. Our contributors share where they found sympathy and empathy and the steps they took to heal and start anew.

The stories were written by or told to us in women's own words. All but two chose to remain anonymous. We edited for clarity, not for content. Some stories may resonate with your experience, others may not. They are all emotional and were part of how women worked through their experience. Some of the content may be upsetting or triggering. If so, take a break.

We offer practical takeaways from each woman's story—concrete suggestions to help you or someone you know or love cope with the immediate aftermath of job loss. We describe everyday strategies for you to consider putting in place, such as having a personal phone in addition to your work phone, so you always have a means of communication that you control. We hope the lessons help spare suffering, save energy, and help women move forward with more confidence, while acknowledging a completely broken system.

Making meaning from endings is largely an individual task, and it is difficult to move on from endings when we cannot give them any meaning. As we experienced and learned about the individual traumas associated with job endings, we came to believe that the current system of termination is broken and cruel. The reality of job endings is rooted in legalese, Human Resources processes and procedures, and outdated expectations. It is as if there is only one way to handle employee "separations," which is to mitigate the theoretical risk to the employer. Legal concerns rule, while human concerns are ignored or negligible at best. This is anything but individual, and it is an event from which it is difficult for anyone to make meaning.

It doesn't have to be this way.

We recognize that companies must change, and restructuring and job transitions are inevitable. And yet, job loss is a topic that is rarely embraced, openly planned for, or discussed within or outside companies. It's just like death! Small wonder that "separations" or "terminations" are rarely done well.

Change begins by exposing a situation or condition that is intolerable.

And so, here we are. To do this, together.

The purpose of this book is to catalyze a public discussion to improve the current reality of job loss by bearing witness[11] to being betrayed by work. It is to share how women lost their jobs, to describe what happened to them immediately and in the aftermath, to validate women's feelings about being fired, and to offer a source of hope and companionship to those of you coping with sudden job loss of your own or of someone you know or love.

We hope to reassure you who are at the crossroads of having lost your job and needing to figure out your next path that you are not alone and you do not have to be without hope. As you will learn from the stories presented here, there turn out to be many entry points to the future for each and every one of you; we hope you will find validation, commonality, and inspiration for them here.

You will notice that many of the women here found and worked with a coach or therapist after they were let go. This book is not intended as a direct advertisement for coaching or therapy, but we noticed that it really seemed to help.

One day soon, we hope that job endings will be openly discussed, understood, and planned for by the employer and employee together. There has to be a better way of ending someone's employment, one that takes account of

---

11   "...bearing witness to the agony of others is itself a soul force." Marianne Williamson, "Bearing Witness to the Agony of Others," *Huffington Post*, 6/21/14 www. huffingtonpost.com/marianne-williamson/bearing-witness_b_5518543.html.

people as human beings with feelings and interconnected relationships. Even though this is not the emphasis of this book, based on the stories offered herein, we offer some preliminary suggestions about how to approach this transaction in Chapter 30. Our primary goal is to communicate to companies and institutions—to all employers—that the moments when they are letting a woman go can have a dramatic and lifelong impact.

Until employers join us with compassion, understanding, and the desire to improve this current reality for all of us, we offer this book to those who have been betrayed by work and experienced the loss of their jobs and careers. To those who didn't see it coming or were blindsided by the unexpected and unthinkable. Your ordeal and its aftermath may have lasted for a longer or shorter time than those described here, but we hope the commonalities and collective voices will be a comfort and an inspiration.

Chapter 1

JULIE: I BUILT SOMETHING WORTH TAKING OVER

A white woman in her mid-forties, Julie was the executive director (CEO) of a well-known nonprofit. She had assembled a top-notch team that built an organization that was very effective in fulfilling its mission.

I knew I was going to be fired.

I was the executive director (CEO) at a nonprofit agency where I had been the leader one month shy of eleven years. I loved my job and was very good at it. I had built a fantastic team and we had grown the organization exponentially, doing great work for our clients. I expected to be there until *I* chose to leave.

I'd just returned to the office after working from home for three months, during and after a difficult hip replacement, and discovered a challenging financial situation. My team and I put together a plan, and I sent an email to my board outlining how we would address the budget while maintaining our services and implementing our new strategic plan.

After receiving my memo, the chairman of the board of directors—a woman—would not return any of my calls or messages, leaving me to intuit that I had somehow transgressed. No other board member returned my call. And when I learned two of my top staff were being questioned by the board, I knew I was in deep trouble. I left a message for the board chair: "If you want me to go, let's discuss it, so we can make it easier for the organization."

At midday on a Wednesday in January, I received a message to go to a board member's office—a lawyer. I knew in my gut that I was going to be fired.

I packed up some personal belongings and walked around the office saying goodbye to people. I told the PR director—someone I had trusted and promoted—that I hoped the board would give me a good severance package because I would cause a stink otherwise. I thought board members would want to avoid negative publicity and handle my departure with dignity. I was wrong. I think she reported my threat to the board, and I believe that angered them.

I was still in pain and using a cane. When I arrived at the fancy building where the board member worked, I was escorted to a bank of elevators and up one floor, where I waited for twenty minutes. I felt disrespected and so afraid. Then, I was escorted, limping, back to the lobby and another bank of elevators to rise many floors. Finally, I hobbled into a conference room occupied by not one, but four board members.

The board chair read a statement I could barely comprehend. Blood was rushing to my head, my heart was pounding, and

I felt nauseous. I asked the chair if I could have a copy of the statement. She looked at the lawyer, who shook her head. I took out a pen and a pad and requested that she repeat the statement so I could take notes. Again, she looked at the lawyer, who nodded. So, I heard again the statement that I was being terminated from my position. No reason was given. I was not permitted to return to the office. My personal belongings would be delivered to me.

I knew they didn't have to give a reason because my state was an "at will" employment state. I wondered if my physical illness and absence had caused the board to lose confidence in my ability to lead.

My head swimming with shock, I declined their offer of car service because I wanted nothing further to do with them. When I reached the train station to go home, I took out my cell phone, only to see that it longer functioned. It was deactivated at the same time I was being fired. I had to hold onto my shock and pain until I reached home and could call someone. At that point, it became the worst day of my life.

I was stunned by what I came to view as a deep betrayal. I didn't deserve such shoddy treatment. I felt as if I were a criminal or persona non grata.

My "departure" generated an article in a major newspaper. I refused to speak to reporters because I didn't want to harm the organization.

I received supportive phone calls from donors and colleagues who were as stunned as I was at my sudden dismissal. People told me mean things board members said, like, "She got too big for her britches." I was so hurt, I said intemperate things. Some people reported everything I said back to the board. I think that closed the members' hearts.

I got a meager severance in light of my long service and success—far less than other chief executives in the nonprofit sector received when they were "terminated"—a month for every year of service. I retained a lawyer and asked for more, as well as for mutual non-disparagement language. My former employer's lawyer refused everything. I had no leverage to get more severance, even though I was over forty and in a protected age class. I couldn't afford to file a discrimination suit based on my health status, plus I would have been labeled a "troublemaker" within the industry and would therefore have become unemployable.

I kept trying to figure out why the board had fired me. Eventually, I deduced it was about power. I believe one member wanted more say in how the organization was run, and, with me gone, he got it. I had developed an organization worth taking over. But I'll never know the reason for sure.

Slowly people stopped calling, and I was on my own. My six-year-old nephew was dying of cancer at this time. The board knew this and still treated me with zero compassion. Perhaps they thought firing me was "business, not personal," but it was intensely personal. Being fired affected my survival. I was a single woman and had to work. I got a short-term consulting contract through my network and began looking for another job. I needed to land something before my severance ran out.

The executive search firm that placed me at my prior executive director job put me up for a prestigious nonprofit

CEO position that seemed like a great fit. The board chair and I agreed on my compensation and a start date of June 1— in the nick of time financially.

On my first day, I stepped off the elevator and thought "this is a mistake." The culture was very different, and my nephew died a month after I started. My grief was so deep, I made some critical relationship missteps. After eight months, the board chair, a lawyer, fired me in a much kinder way. I got a decent severance, was allowed to pack up my things, and said goodbye to people. I left the organization in far better shape than when I started.

Once again, I searched for an ED/CEO job. The search consultant said it would be hard for me to get something because I'd been fired twice. That sparked enormous fear. I did get interviews from curiosity-seekers. I got to the final round for a job leading a new organization in California, but it didn't meet my minimum salary requirement. I got depressed and anxious, but knew I had to keep putting one foot in front of the other. Eventually, I would find a job.

Then, out of the blue, I had to have back surgery and became physically disabled. Now what? Fortunately, I had disability insurance, which gave me income and breathing room to figure out next steps.

I slowly realized I was not going to be a nonprofit executive director again. Too many rejections and my physical limitations made it clear that this path was now closed.

To satisfy a long-standing desire for a graduate degree, I got an MBA in leadership. It turned out that I already knew 80 percent of what I studied, which was validating. I added to my credentials and rebuilt my damaged self-esteem.

I asked myself, "What is my new path?" I tried a few things: consulting, selling jewelry, doing research, writing proposals. None clicked. So I looked at what I loved to do, and what really made me happy. This was my "must have" list: I had to be able to do it via the telephone, computer, and the internet. I had to interact with and help other people. I needed varied, intellectually stimulating, and challenging work. I had to be able to gradually ramp up earnings and get off disability.

I'd learned that, when I was clear about what I wanted, I would manifest it. So I wrote everything down and got to work taking action.

I joined a local job seekers' group that helped me handle the emotional trauma of being fired. We read *Transitions* by William Bridges,[12] which helped me heal. I came to see that I could not begin a new phase without ending the previous one, and that I would go through a "neutral zone" of being neither here nor there, but in ambiguity.

I volunteered to host a "Monday Morning Get-Going" meeting for group members. I found myself guiding the conversation and coaching people informally. I loved helping people find what they love to do. Could I become a career coach? I knew coaching worked, because I'd had a coach for twelve years. I had worked in workforce development, studied coaching, and conducted successful job hunts, including finding my

---

12   Transitions: Making Sense of Life's Choices, William Bridges. Revised Anniversary Edition, Da Capo Lifelong Books, 2019. See also The Way of Transition: Embracing Life's Most Difficult Moments, William Bridges. Da Capo Lifelong Books, 2001.

"right fit" work as a nonprofit leader. I could help others who had experienced the humiliation and dissonance of being fired. I realized I wanted to help other people find their "right fit" work.

To gain experience, I offered free coaching by phone to anyone willing to be my guinea pig. My first client was a woman in Brooklyn. I lived on disability and savings while I developed my system for coaching. I connected with people in the job search/career coaching world through Twitter and LinkedIn. I blogged about job search and developed a following.

I hadn't intended to start my own business. But I had run two nonprofit businesses, and I couldn't see myself working for anyone else.

Eventually, I ended my reliance on disability, even though I wondered if I could really support myself. I recommitted to my coaching business, charged more, and trusted that I would be okay. So far, so good.

Support from friends and family was essential to my healing. We shared anger and sorrow, as well as grieving my nephew. I reconnected with a therapist to process these huge losses. I went to what I call "personal development university" where I learned about myself, moved out of fear, and became a better me. I have two coaches and benefit greatly from their wisdom and validation that my work is of value.

I am not one who says getting fired was a good thing. It wasn't. It was unbearably painful. I lost so much—my identity, my income, my ability to effect positive change in the world, and for a while, my path. I had to overcome thinking I was to blame for the way I was treated. I accept responsibility for my actions while knowing I didn't cause board members to behave in any way—I am not that powerful.

Nonetheless, I found positive aspects of having been fired. I no longer had to be "on" almost always, wondering who would recognize me or turn out to be a donor. Such hypervigilance was exhausting and possibly contributed to my health problems. I also am glad to be free of a board of directors. Every nonprofit CEO I've talked to or coached complains about their board. Boards control the CEO's fate yet are largely unaware of what it takes to lead a complex business serving essential human needs.

I now believe I had to leave that environment to fully embrace my purpose in life. It took years to accept that "God did for me what I could not do for myself." I wish it had not been so painful an experience, and I believe that it did not have to be.

Carrying feelings of resentment and anger around hurt me. So I forgave the board members and staff who did their best, although their best wasn't very good.

I love what I do now. I work virtually with clients all over the US and in other parts of the world, getting clients mainly through referrals. I can be myself every day, sharing my experience and expertise to help others find their path to satisfying work. My work matters, too, because people who are happy at work can be happy in the rest of their lives, and this can ripple far beyond them.

POSTSCRIPT

Julie is a successful executive/career coach and organizational development consultant. She has translated her experience into helping others have successful careers.

PRACTICAL TAKEAWAYS

- If you think you are getting "the Call" from HR or your boss, bring paper and pen to the meeting to record what's said to you.

- Forgive yourself if you become volatile when you get the news that you are fired. Your "fight or flight" survival instinct has been activated, which is beyond your control.[13]

- You may never figure out the real reason why you were fired; you can still move on.

- Treat yourself with compassion and dignity, so termination does not destroy your self-confidence and identity.

- It may take a few tries to find your path, as you may need to "try things on" to see if they "fit."

---

13   See Goleman, Daniel, Emotional Intelligence: Why It Can Matter More Than IQ, NY: Bantam Books, 1995; Goleman, D., Boyatsis, R., McKee, A. (2013). Primal Leadership: Unleashing the Power of Emotional Intelligence. Boston, MA: Harvard Business Institute; Hamilton, Diane Musho, "Calming Your Brain During Conflict," Harvard Business Review, December 22, 2015 hbr.org/2015/12/calming-your-brain-during-conflict.

Chapter 2

KAYLA: I TEXTED "THERE IS ONE LESS BLACK GIRL ON WALL STREET TODAY"

Kayla, a Black woman in her mid-thirties, had risen in the financial technology field. Her new white male boss made her working life difficult, yet her boss's boss and the HR director were only interested in how she could improve the working relationship.

I was fired the week before Thanksgiving, right before I turned forty. I had a one-year-old at home and had worked successfully at the same company for seven years. But, because my boss didn't like me, I was fired from my job.

I was Vice President of Client Services for a large trading fintech firm. I loved my job and had a really good reputation on Wall Street. My job allowed me to use the skills I had developed from trading while not actually trading, which made me happy. I traveled quite a bit, which I enjoyed. I was happy at the firm and was promoted every year I worked there.

Then, things changed. I became pregnant, which was great news! My life seemed to be falling into order. However, I was over thirty-five, and, because of an incident in the firm's lobby where a woman pushed me, my doctor barred me from traveling. While my manager was fine with me utilizing technology to serve my clients (who were also fine with it), we were in the midst of a reorganization, and my new manager was a man I had a not-so-great history with.

He had harassed me in front of a client about deliverables the client had already received. He had also gone to management and insisted that he be in my client meetings, despite this deviating from protocol. In the meeting where he challenged the work already done, he spoke over me and acted out so terribly that the client demanded he never be allowed back and wrote a letter to our CEO to that effect. This man made the firm look bad and almost damaged my relationship with that client. I felt I had no choice but to complain to his superior. This led to arbitration, which ended in my favor. Suffice to say, I was not one of his favorite people.

I didn't understand why he was chosen to be manager of my group when he had no relevant experience and had been confrontational with one of its star members (me). But I made sure not to show him any visible disrespect and instead focused on how I could best serve my clients. It was getting closer to my maternity leave, and with the help of my team, I was able to make sure all work was done via phone and WebEx. There was still the open issue of who would cover my clients once I was on leave.

I set up meetings with my new manager to discuss who would handle which clients, but he kept cancelling. I introduced a few of my clients to trusted colleagues who could assist them in my absence and let them know that my manager would reach out before I went on leave. He never did, though. And my son arrived three weeks early, exactly fifteen hours after my last hour at work.

So, for the first month of my maternity leave, I responded to my clients' emails because my manager ignored them. I never thought to complain, as I trusted he would get around to assigning clients. Instead *he* went to HR and complained that I was responding to clients. Human Resources called me, asking that I not respond to clients during my maternity leave. I complied.

My agreed-upon maternity leave was for three months, with the understanding that, once I returned, I would work at home two days and in the office three days a week. My manager wanted to change that immediately. He constantly made snide comments about how I could not go out after work because I had to do the mommy thing. He reprimanded me for not attending a last-minute meeting in Philadelphia when my husband was in surgery, even though I attended it virtually. He tried to write me up, but my client had already written to the company's managing director, saying he had confused the date of my husband's surgery and was happy that I had attended at all.

When I returned to the office full-time, the relationship with my manager got worse. He insisted on going to all my client meetings, claiming he went to client meetings with other VPs. This was false (I asked them). Not coincidentally, they were all men and I was the lone woman, and a Black woman at that.

I think he was intimidated by my competence. He came to one of my client meetings and spent the majority of the time stating inaccuracies, which ended with the client calling him out as not knowing what he was talking about. He took on one of the softball clients, meaning he only had to do easy five-minute reporting and twenty-minute meetings, once a quarter. But he lacked the skill to do the report. I sat with him to explain the work, but, after two quarters, I just did the reports for him.

I saw the writing on the wall. I believed he was building a case to get rid of me. So, I began amassing evidence on my own behalf and went to HR to say he was harassing me. Their response was to ask what I could do to make this relationship work better. I replied that "I could be less Black and not a woman, because other colleagues—men—come in late and it's no big deal, but I leave for ten minutes to retrieve breast milk from the refrigerator and I'm harassed for days at a time." HR agreed to talk to him.

Unfortunately, he got more aggressive. I had a lot of stress every day, not knowing what he would accuse me of next. He told me that I didn't know how to use the product we provided to clients, when I had taught *him* how to use the product. I'll never forget the day he screamed at me, "I demand you be respectful of me!" I said to him, "My father doesn't scream at me."

In October, I had to go to HR to hear my boss's complaints about me. HR and my boss wanted me to acknowledge that he was writing me up. I refused.

I left the office right away and went to the Equal Employment Opportunity Commission offices, to investigate whether I had a basis for a claim. By this time, I had a lot of information about everything he didn't do, such as meetings with me he blew off, "read receipts" for emails he had read, yet claimed he hadn't received, and more.

I would go to work and at lunch would go to the EEOC. I began to have anxiety attacks. I was falling apart at home and at work. One day, in a snowstorm, I sat crying on the steps of an outdoor plaza. In a moment of sanity, I called a friend to come get me.

My grandmother told me that people are going to test you, and you just have to move forward and ignore those people. Black women get that message. It's a dangerous message, because it does not allow us to feel, to vent, to speak—no matter the cost.

Leading up to my being fired, I had been in several meetings with the managing director regarding the team's work. This particular meeting was supposed to be just him and me, but my boss and another colleague were also there. I made my presentation, and jokingly said to the managing director (MD), "I see you set me up by having the other two people there." He seemed to respond in kind and assured me that I had done a good job. But a week later, I got a call from the head of HR, who wanted to make sure I was okay. I didn't understand what he meant. He said he had heard that I had a confrontation with the MD. I told him that I was okay, I had been joking. But I realized that now both the MD and my manager saw me as a problem. I had to look for another job.

Two weeks later, I had a feeling. The day started like every other stressful day. About ten o'clock, I was summoned to the MD's office. He sat behind his desk. The head of HR stood to the left at the window. My manager sat in a chair against the wall, behind me. An empty chair in front of the desk was for me. The MD said, "It seems like you and your manager will never get along." I agreed. He continued, "So we've decided to terminate the relationship. We'll give you severance, insurance intact for a length of time. Do you have any questions?" I said "No." He asked how I was feeling, and I said, "I feel like I should go right now." He said, "It was a pleasure working with you." I responded, "The first five years were a great experience, but the last two years were terrible, and you didn't help."

He asked my manager to get my bag from my desk. I responded, "I am capable of getting my own bag, and he wouldn't know my bag if it hit him in the face." A security guard walked with me to my desk, then rode down with me. When I handed him my badge, he said, "When they said Kayla, I thought it was someone else. I was so shocked it was you." I left the building and texted my friends, "There's one less Black girl on Wall Street today and you can meet me at the bar." And I went immediately to the EEOC. I called a few clients from there. One said, "If you're no longer there, we're no longer there," which made me feel great.

The first day was hard, the second day was harder, and the third day was even harder. I went from shock to overwhelm. *What do I do now? Make a resume? Do a job search? Where do I go?* Self-blame came up. I had put so much into that place because I thought I could succeed there. *I did my job, so why did I get fired?* Someone took a dislike to me and decided it was easier to harass me and get me out. I didn't quit, so he had to orchestrate me out. I got really angry then.

I filed a race- and sex-based claim with the EEOC against my firm, and the EEOC served the company with papers regarding an investigation into my claim. The company already had several EEOC violations.

After EEOC served them, the HR head called me under the guise of wanting to know if I had questions, saying, "We've always been friends." Then he asked if I would help them investigate the claims I made against my manager. I was shocked and angry! I asked, "You want me to help you investigate the man who harassed me for two years? Why? So another woman doesn't suffer?" I went on, "I wasn't important to you. You had all the facts, and instead you chose to fire me. So, no, I won't help you."

The company ended up quickly settling my claim and I received a larger severance package. That helped financially, but the damage they did to my spirit still lingers, daily. The entire experience was really traumatic for me. I did get another job but couldn't start it for a year, because my anxiety went on that long.

It's really challenging for Black women in finance. There are so few of us and so little support for being yourself. I love the field and I do my job well, but I'm really cautious now about putting too much of myself into my work. I have two wonderful boys, and a great husband. I have begun writing again about the inequality Black women face in the corporate world, which I enjoy doing and focus on daily.

POSTSCRIPT

Telling her story for this book helped Kayla heal and was the nudge she needed to create a comic telling her stories of the microaggressions Black women face in the workplace, which are essentially macro aggressions.

PRACTICAL TAKEAWAYS

- Getting fired can ruin your feelings of self-worth, so don't be surprised if you feel that way.

- Develop a daily routine when you are between jobs, so you have some structure and things to look forward to.

- Keep private copies of your meaningful contacts outside the workplace.

- Know the system at your employer and learn what you are entitled to get, and what you need to do to get it.

Chapter 3

JILL: I HAD NEVER BEEN FIRED SO MANY TIMES IN ONE WEEK

A white woman in her early fifties, Jill was a personal training coach with multiple jobs. When COVID-19 hit, she was incredibly vulnerable.

I was the head coach at a gym. COVID-19 affected all gyms in the area.

I have been a personal training coach for about fifteen years and had been at this gym for about seven years.

Becoming a coach for this gym was one of the hardest trainings I have ever done, and I have been an athlete since college. It was incredibly intense and in a different element (land) than my preferred one (water). There were blisters and pain, and it was just really hard. I am proud of this accomplishment.

The day I was fired was crazy. The night before, I taught the last class of the day and, it turned out, the last class offered, period.

Three days earlier, my husband began to suspect this would happen, so he advised me to apply for unemployment before everyone started doing it at once. I took his advice and got set up.

Now we were on a Zoom call that wasn't working properly. Everyone (staff and coaches) was on the call and it was utter chaos...people were saying, *What?*

I can't hear, what's happening?

What's going on?

And then the word started to circulate.

He's firing everyone.

My Zoom wasn't working, so another coach was texting me what was going on. Even though I had sort of expected it and wasn't upset, per se, I was stunned that it was conducted in such a messy way.

After the call was over, I told a coach friend to register for unemployment immediately. Another coach who was a manager called everyone individually to say this was a temporary arrangement so people could collect unemployment, and everyone would be welcomed back once the studio reopened.

In other words, *See ya when we see ya.*

None of us heard a peep from the owners after we were fired, en masse, on that Zoom call.

The fellow who trained me to be a trainer told me to never put all my eggs in one basket. He told me, you might have a great following, but one day you'll show up and the gym is closed because of drugs being found or money being stolen or a health reason and suddenly you're out of a job. He pointed out that gym franchises have a high coach turnover rate, sometimes to keep everything fresh and interesting.

I kept that in mind when I started at this gym. The place smelled like desperation. So I worked when the owners were not there to avoid the stress and micromanagement they were well known for.

For a long time, I was the only woman trainer. My classes were always full: some people followed me from other gyms, while others naturally gravitated to me and my classes. I like this kind of work, and I am confident when training and motivating people. Some people would only work with me.

But get this: to generate business, the owners decided to bring in the press to film the gym and clients working out. However, they didn't want a woman trainer in the images. They also didn't want me to find that out. So they set up the press interview when I was away, had a male coach teach my classes, and put the word out to keep this little effort quiet. Of course, I found out, and my husband got a free membership at the gym for a year.

I did not put all my eggs in this basket. I also had individual clients I was training regularly. I ran a summer kids' swimming program. The parents of those kids knew me and trusted me. I also worked with the elderly and led group fitness classes at another local fitness center for about eleven years. At that center, I trained benefactors on the board of directors as well as staff, and I brought in money, so I had a lot of freedom in my routine.

Unlike the owner who fired us over Zoom, the boss of the other fitness center didn't immediately close it. So the Thursday before everything with COVID started to unravel our lives, I said to one of my classes, *Ladies, if we are still open, if you feel safe, I will be here for you.*

However, once it became clear what was happening with COVID, all my work came to a halt almost overnight. Suddenly there was no work in my field—or for me.

I felt like I had never been fired so many times in just one week!

Part of me was delighted to be home. I got unemployment, including the extra six hundred dollars a week. The government wanted me to stay home and pay me? I thought, "That's great, I haven't had a summer off in ages!!" Going from 110 miles per hour to zero mph took a little getting used to, of course. My to-do list was almost done within two months.

As it went on, COVID was rough on me as an athlete and a coach. I didn't have the motivation to do anything—to show up myself to be trained. I worked out on one day. I know how to train myself to get back into shape, but I just didn't have the energy or desire. Doing nothing, or feeling like I could do nothing, made me nuts. A body at rest stays at rest. One day, I baked cupcakes with a chocolate buttercream whipped icing. Per instructions from the internet, I cut a tip from a Ziplock bag and piped the icing onto the cupcakes, and they looked great. That's about all I could do.

Spring 2020 weather was horrible—freezing and rainy. I did not want to go outside to work out.

My husband has health problems, and his boss kept him on partial employment status so he kept his health benefits. We have tenants in a home we own and had to work with each tenant separately to figure out what they needed and how to meet the expenses of the house. I asked for deferred payments from our creditors.

So many of our gym members are front-line people working at local hospitals, and I don't know how they are. I wonder, when we get back, who is not going to be there.

The gym was my outlet. It was a way to take a break from the challenging situation of my husband's health. One of the reasons I like coaching is that it's unfiltered. Anyone can break down and cry at any point of the workout, so it is real. This was my therapy, my savior. No matter what kind of day I was having at home, I realized I could forget it when I was working with other people.

The people at the gym had some Zoom happy hours, where we got to see each other and that was nice. We were so used to seeing each other and working together regularly in a dynamic, energetic environment, that it made the COVID isolation even harder.

I am older than many folks at the gym. I worry about my levels of fitness, especially given that it's been hard to stay motivated to work out during COVID. My husband said he didn't want me giving online classes at one point, which held me back from potential job opportunities. Then he changed his tune and said it was okay for me to teach online. That made me mad!

In terms of how COVID will unfold from here, not one person will come out of this unscathed. I know it's changed my life. I do not know what the gym will be like, how many trainers will be there, or how many people will be training. Some people may not want to train any more, period. Maybe my private clients won't want to train. I still want to work with older people.

In terms of moving forward after COVID, well, I have reinvented myself numerous times and realize I may have to do it again. As women, sometimes we don't see that maybe we worked for a company where we could only go so far because we are women.

It is true that when one door closes, another one opens. It's so easy to look backward to see how this works. You have to have faith that, whether through your education or your life experience or knowing somebody who will support you, there will always be opportunities, if you are willing to work for them.

Anyway, I am confident in myself and my abilities, and I will say that being a personal coach brought that out of me. I love having variety in my life, because I believe that doing the same thing every day will make me old. I also have learned that we do what we need to do when we need to pay the bills.

Someone told me I have a wonderful, wide-ranging influence because I touch so many people in so many different areas of life. I am extremely honest in my communication with people. I try to be transparent because, if you're not honest, it will hurt you in the end. I was one of the people who brought the most people into the gym and, when one of the owners asked me how I was doing it, I told her that I told people it was cheaper than therapy. Which is 100 percent true.

Two last things, about the firing. A few days after we were all fired, a friend pointed out that the owner didn't have to fire us, but he did. I train someone who owns another franchise. She tried to hang on to her employees and keep them paid for as long as possible. By the time she was forced to close, it was harder for people to register for unemployment. There were no good options in COVID.

The most hurtful part about this is that the owner's true colors came out. He didn't contact anyone personally, which reveals a lot about him. I finally sent him a text saying it would be nice for him to reach out to all the coaches and see how they are doing. He replied by thanking me for being me. I was really disappointed when he sent everyone a generic text message. He showed not one iota of care—it felt like he is not human. This guy owns the rights for a successful gym franchise in the area and is essentially unhappy because he is not making millions this month. Based on being treated like this, it is not clear how many of us are motivated to return. But the big picture is that, right now, there is no smog, there are whales and dolphins returning to some of the coastal areas, and maybe the break the world is taking will make it better.

POSTSCRIPT

Jill conducted personal training sessions outdoors using COVID-19 safety precautions and is now training indoors again.

PRACTICAL TAKEAWAYS

- File for unemployment the moment you are fired, regardless of how you feel; you paid into it, so you earned it.

- You can choose to "act as if" and be positive even during a difficult time.

- How you get fired is a true reflection of how much the employer values you—or not.

Chapter 4

BIRDIE: I BRISTLED WHEN SOMEONE SAID, "DON'T WORRY, HONEY"

Birdie, a white woman in her early fifties, worked in government. A change in administration usually didn't mean changes for her.

I was let go over a period of about nine months.

In politics, you can lose your job based on what party gets voted into or out of office. However, I had been in my position for over twenty years—across parties and administrations—because I was competent, capable, and nice to people.

Then a new politician from the same party came to power. Let me tell you, these people ate their own. They got rid of all of my previous boss's people. The new staff were awful to me but expected me to share my carefully cultivated database and teach them what I did.

The first thing they did was do away with my assistant's position without telling her or me in advance. One day she called me, frantic, and, when I called the Secretary of the administration, they told me, "Oh yes, that position is being done away with."

Next, I didn't get my rehiring paperwork, so I kept calling and asking for it. The rumor was that there was a list of people they were going to fire. Instead of firing me, they moved me to another building. They called me at four o'clock and said I had to be out by nine o'clock the next morning. I had already packed half my stuff because I had a feeling something was going to happen. I packed until six thirty and was ready for the movers at nine thirty the next morning.

I continued to do my job in my new office. I was in a no-person's-land with no one around me, but I had a great view and didn't have to see these people every day.

A few months later, I was called by the HR director, who said there was an internal investigation and I was on the list of people they wanted to talk to. I said I wasn't going in there without an attorney, and I found one who coached me through the meeting.

The investigator told me that my position was not in jeopardy; they were investigating a woman bullying other employees, including me. I spoke truth to power and said yes, I had been bullied by this woman and told the investigators about my experience with her. It seemed like they were compiling evidence to get rid of her—my lawyer told me I had done everything right.

Unfortunately, as I learned later, she was on the inside, had the ear of the new leader, and wanted my position.

One month later, I was let go at 10:05 a.m. The HR director came into my office and closed my door. I thought, "Oh, this is not good." She had been doing my time and attendance for the previous nine months, and I knew I was being watched.

I wasn't too worried, because I was usually the last one to leave the office and it was widely recognized that I was dedicated and a hard worker.

The HR director was shaking and simply stated over and over, "Your services are no longer needed." I felt like I was in a dream—it was an out-of-body experience. I was shaking. I wondered if it had been in response to the investigation. I kept asking why, and that was all she would say.

She helped me pack up and told me I had to get back on the payroll within a year to retain my benefits. I was twenty-two months away from retiring with a full pension. People were not allowed to take their Rolodexes with them, but I had personal information there. It was twenty-plus years' worth of work, and I took my Rolodex. When someone is fired, a Sergeant at Arms escorts the person out. It's horribly embarrassing, and it makes you feel like a criminal. I asked her, "Are you going to have the sergeant come over and escort me out like I'm a criminal?" and she said, "No, I'm not going to do that to you."

The maintenance guys put everything in my convertible Volkswagen Bug. I had them take a picture of me in my car with my stuff. And then I drove home.

I had a friend come over for lunch. Other friends came over, and I just kept on going until around midnight. Then I broke down.

The next day, an article in a state newspaper about all the people who were fired that day—it wasn't just me—made me sound incompetent. The politician did this on purpose to make sure I wouldn't get hired again in government. I still don't understand why he did that.

Every night, I was scared. I would wake up in the night, thinking, worried about how to find a job, how to go on interviews, how to keep my house. At that point I didn't have any money coming in and that was terrifying, especially since the COBRA plan was hundreds of dollars a month. I had to dip into my deferred compensation just to live. Some days, I didn't want to get out of bed.

I started looking for work right away. The wonderful women I used as references to get my job called me immediately once they heard the story and asked how they could help. I said I needed a job within the government because I had to get back on payroll to keep my retirement benefits.

I had an immediate job offer two weeks after being let go but thought it was not a good fit. I listened to my gut. A lot of people wanted to meet with me, so I felt like I would find something.

At first, I would go to the library every day because I didn't have a computer. I gave my resume to everyone and applied for everything that would get me back on payroll. After a lot of phone calls, I found out there would be a 17 percent cut in my retirement benefits if I didn't get back on payroll.

I did go to the unemployment office. It felt weird and smelled weird and the first thing I saw was a photograph of a well-known staircase that I used to walk up every day on my way to work. It made me want to throw up. I used to be there, and now I'm here, just a number. I'll never forget that moment.

The unemployment counselors were great. They helped me find a temporary job at the State Police. Everyone there had lost a previous job. Hearing their stories and sharing mine with them was helpful and reassuring. When I was there, one guy got a full-time job, and we celebrated. I used a sergeant there as one of my references for my next job. He was nice (and handsome!).

Having a temporary job got me out of the house and seeing people. I found a free local gym and met nice women there. By this point, I had a routine: I would get up, have coffee, get on the computer (I had one by now), go to the gym, shop at the grocery store, and then look for work, or go to work. But I was totally stressed out because there was only a certain amount of time to get back on the payroll.

I found my next job on a website, a receptionist position. I was a nervous wreck when I interviewed for it. I hadn't interviewed for a job in years, and a lot had changed in twenty years! Over four hundred people applied for the position, and they only interviewed me. The people in the government agency knew my story and knew I wasn't going to be there very long, which also worked for them.

I took the job and a $40,000 pay cut just so I could get back into the payroll system. I worked as a receptionist for two years until I could retire. When I left, my boss said, "You were a really good fit, and I hate to see you go."

One day, I answered the phone, and it was the previous Head Counsel for the politician. He was surprised that I was there. He went out of his way to say he had nothing to do with how

I was treated. I told him they knew exactly what they were doing, and it was wrong.

When I retired, I got everything back that they tried to take away from me: my benefits, my sick time, and my retirement.

I later learned that the HR director said that firing me was the hardest thing she ever did. People wanted to pick my brain after I was let go, and I decided that I wasn't telling anybody anything. Use Google.

To me, the most hurtful part was the financial part. When you are older, it's hard to find a job. It was on my mind all the time. Somebody said, "Birdie just needs to get over it." I got so angry!! How can you get over it? This was my livelihood. They financially hurt me and they did it on purpose. People did hurtful things to me for their own personal gain.

Getting fired ruins your feelings of self-worth. I felt like smelly trash. I kept wondering, *Was I not smart? Did I not deserve to have a job?* It was awful. This experience—these feelings—will always be close to me.

The person who bullied me was eventually let go, and at one point I called her and asked if she was behind me getting fired—what did I have to lose? She said, absolutely not.

I had a good circle of friends around me who kept encouraging me and reminding me that God is good. I hid my feelings and tried to stay positive. I encourage other women to always stay positive, even in your darkest hour. You have to keep going. Drink after five o'clock, not before. Make sure you get up every morning and get a routine.

My parents were super supportive. They had both worked in politics and knew the game. They were both mad. My brother was not supportive. He would say "Get a job yet?" when I saw him. And when I got a job, it was only a quick "Congratulations."

My biggest takeaway from this experience is that there is no such thing as job security. If people want to get rid of you, they will. There is no loyalty any longer in the work world. They can dispose of you, and, truthfully, they could care less about you. I wish I could have initiated a lawsuit against that politician and his minions, but I needed to get back onto the state payroll, and no one would have hired me if I had done that.

There should be a way to give notice that the job is coming to an end. Give people some transition time to get their affairs in order and to get another job. It seems like that would be a better way of doing things than what someone said to me at the time, which was, "Don't worry, honey. You're a smart lady, you'll find something." This was a horrible event in my life, but I survived it, and I learned.

POSTSCRIPT

Birdie retired with her full pension and took some time for herself to think about what to do next. Now she works part-time in a job that enables her to keep active and see people that she knew before.

PRACTICAL TAKEAWAYS

- Getting fired can ruin your feelings of self-worth, so don't be surprised if you feel that way.

- Develop a daily routine when you are between jobs, so you have some structure and things to look forward to.

- Keep private copies of your meaningful contacts outside of the workplace.

- Know the system at your employer and learn what you are entitled to get, and what you need to do to get it.

Chapter 5

NICOLE: I GOT MY CONFIDENCE BACK

Nicole, a Black woman in her late thirties, worked in the advertising industry, where it was common for people to be laid off when clients changed agencies. Disagreements with clients were not only usual but were considered to be part of the job.

I was fired twice.

It's not uncommon in my industry, but both times felt terrible, especially the first time. Right around the end-of-year holidays, the media agency I worked at did a round of layoffs because they lost some accounts.

My boss called me into a meeting, and two other senior leaders were there as well. She told me a client had asked that I leave their account due to a disagreement, and there was no other account for me to work on. She said she wished I had brought this situation to her attention earlier so she could have helped, but now it had progressed too far for her to be able to do anything to help. She said they would offer me a package and left me alone with the person from HR.

I was shocked and practically speechless. I asked the person from HR if I could have some time before I signed anything, and they agreed. I went to my locker (we had an open floor plan with no assigned desks), got my things, and left. Thankfully, no one escorted me out.

This was a big blow to my confidence. There's a lot of ego in advertising, but also camaraderie. We're all in the trenches together, so when we win an account or the client likes a campaign, we celebrate together.

Being fired was painful.

I thought: *You've sent me to the UK and Denmark on new biz pitches, I've helped you win business, and you like me! How could you fire me?!!*

I am super competitive and felt like I lost.

As the shock wore off, I got upset. My boss didn't have my back! She didn't give me any opportunity to make the situation right with the client. Even though we had disagreed, I had no idea the client was this unhappy. I thought our disagreements were par for the course. But my boss dumped me without any chance to explain, while I thought we understood each other.

Second, I knew there were plenty of other accounts I could have been placed on. If I'd been white, I think she would have been more apt to find a place for me. I've seen many white account executives removed from one account and put on another. White males especially. But, instead, she chose to fire me.

At ad agencies, you get typecast. Most want, and I quote, a *minority* in the group photo and in the room for the business pitch and client meetings, so it looks like the agency is diverse. But most of the actual service is performed by older white men—they are the copywriters and art directors.

There's not much of a role for older Black women in advertising agencies unless you become the head of Diversity and Inclusion. There's a lot more scope and freedom for white people.

It was hard to tell my husband that I had been let go. He was also working, so financially, it wasn't a big deal (we could manage), but it was a surprise. I felt like I got a decent package—six weeks of severance. My friends and my career coach helped me get through the self-esteem issues and own my abilities. I got super into rock-climbing. It was something I could be good at, and I was good at.

It took me two to three months to find my next job. I networked constantly and updated my LinkedIn profile; recruiters got in touch, and eventually I landed my next job. It was a good fit. I got a jump in title and pay and enjoyed the people I worked with, even though the location was far from where I live (which meant a commute).

A former coworker said my former boss was tight-lipped about what happened. I also didn't bad-mouth her or the agency because it's a small industry and I didn't want to burn bridges. I was glad she didn't bad-mouth me.

The second time I was fired, it was from an agency that was a total cultural miss. They recruited me from my second job (the one I found initially after I was fired), they offered a big bump in pay and title, and they were located much closer to where I live. All good, right?

I joined in late November and, almost immediately, my boss was out for two months due to a surgery. When she returned, she heard only negative feedback about me: my colleagues didn't like how I worked with them.

To wit: At larger agencies, there is a lot of collaboration, and you don't have to present a fully fleshed-out campaign to get feedback from your colleagues. Feedback is fast and not terribly polite because time's a tickin'. We had pretty thick skins because we understood the model and what we were supposed to do.

Not so at this agency. People wanted everything buttoned up and polished, as if our own colleagues were the client. This agency had grown by acquiring smaller agencies. As such, there hadn't been much effort toward creating a single agency culture, vocabulary, and set of practices. As a result of there not being a big-agency, many-voice culture, I didn't mesh well.

It was strange, even from the start. I didn't have anyone reporting to me, although I was a senior vice president. I wasn't asked to be on big projects or participate in any meaningful way. And, as I was not meshing well, I was pretty sure I'd be let go soon. In fact, I had already started clearing out my desk.

The agency didn't want to pay the recruiter who brought me in, so they fired me within three months. The day it happened, my boss called me in, and, after some general greetings and checking in, said I should go to someone else's office for the second half of the meeting. Yeah, I sensed something was definitely up. When I arrived at the next office, I saw someone I didn't recognize, who was introduced as being from HR. My boss then went into the feedback she'd received, namely, that I criticized other teams, that I didn't recognize other people's contributions, that my style was abrasive and abrupt, and that I presented work in progress instead of finished work.

To me, it seemed like a massive misunderstanding. But I didn't argue. I didn't want to stay there. There was no leadership or guidance, and I didn't get assigned a mentor as promised. The firm was supposed to have a great thirty/sixty/ninety-day structured onboarding program, but none of that took place.

The people I was supposed to work with weren't really coworkers, they were resentful employees of acquired companies. It felt like a mean girls' club!

Someone went to my desk, got my jacket, came back, and then walked me to the elevator. There wasn't anyone I wanted to say goodbye to.

I was fired right before the COVID-19 quarantine hit. The timing was great, because I was fired before anyone else lost their jobs due to COVID-19. I didn't have to fight to get unemployment; it came right away. I also got the extra six hundred dollars a week.

Financially, we were okay for a while. But because my husband had retired by this time, I needed to go back to work fast. Again, I did the usual networking and applying for jobs, talking to recruiters, etc. I had a lot of phone interviews in the first four to six weeks, but things died down as the pandemic progressed. I started to get worried about when or if things would pick up for me. We had been thinking about moving, so I started to look at jobs in different cities.

But, in the spring, I joined Chief, a private network focused on connecting and supporting women leaders. My SVP title from the last job helped me get accepted. I wanted to explore changing careers and get insight from women who were more experienced and in positions higher than mine. I was especially interested in how they approached jobs, negotiated compensation, and got promotions.

It took me five months to find another job. I got to enjoy my kids, to help them with school, to go to the park with them, and to be a parent. I recovered my confidence by volunteering to do work I enjoy, by helping a friend of my mom with her lupus nonprofit and by helping a local group. I did some good work!

In late spring, I was contacted through LinkedIn by a chief strategy officer at an agency about a role they had not yet posted. I interviewed with her and then with another woman who had worked in some of the same places I had. Very quickly, the two offered me a freelance position as a senior vice president, with the intention of the job becoming permanent. I was nervous about accepting the offer because I was nervous about having women bosses again.

I've had one great woman boss that I looked up to and learned from, but other women bosses fired me. I think they were insecure and didn't understand how I worked. Even though they never complained about the outcome or result, they still felt the need to nitpick. I didn't appreciate that.

I look back and see that that's how I got in trouble with a previous client; he tried to tell me *how* to do my work.

Nevertheless, I took the position, and am really happy. I have a great title at a great agency—a big global agency. It's going well. I'm not full-time, but I'm being introduced to clients. My bosses compliment me a lot and have repeated that they want me to come on full-time when possible. I have dotted-line reports; I help organize their thinking, and I talk them through client presentations.

One really great thing is that there are Black people who are active and visible in this agency. I don't think there are numerically more Black people than in other agencies, per se, but the issues of diversity are openly discussed at workshops, in white papers, and in discussions with leadership. One Black SVP who was exiting the company contacted me when he found out I had been hired and gave me the lay of the land, who the allies were and who was cold. He also set up meetings for me with different people. Now, when I'm on a call with senior leaders and my boss, some of the leaders know me because of him. My boss is impressed.

I don't think my career has been negatively affected by racism, but I don't know what my career trajectory would have been if I hadn't been fired the first time.

Did I want to stay at that agency anyway?

No. I don't want to work for someone who doesn't have my back.

I've certainly experienced instances of racism and microaggressions in the advertising world. For instance, if a

Black person from a completely different department leaves my company, white people will ask me why he left. I didn't know him, so how would I know why he left?

Or someone will ask me for my opinion, as if I speak for all Black people. There's a special ignorance that you get accustomed to. For instance, I'm comfortable saying something when Creative is skewing white, like showing golfers—a very white sport—in something they are trying to convey, because that choice (golf) is just not effective in reaching a broad audience.

The most important thing I've learned is to understand how others navigate your industry. I accepted things I didn't have to accept in terms of employment and bonuses. I now know to negotiate the terms of my departure when I'm hired: you never have more leverage than when they want you. I've ended in a much better place, so for me, I learned that it's not the end to be fired.

POSTSCRIPT

Nicole enjoys her work today, as she applies some of the lessons she's learned from her own and other women's experiences. She spends more time with her family and is making more connections in her women's network.

PRACTICAL TAKEAWAYS

- Ask for time before signing any separation documents so you have a clear head.

- If you have an employment contract for your next job, negotiate your departure terms when you begin, when you have the most leverage because they want you.

- Spend some time studying and understanding the "vibe" of your office, so you don't ruffle feathers unnecessarily.

Chapter 6

JENNIFER: I DISCOVERED MY VOICE

Jennifer, a white woman in her mid-forties, was a registered nurse who did her job when she refused to comply with a request by the supervisor that she knew could have resulted in the loss of her license.

It was not the first layoff I had experienced in my profession, but it was definitely the most traumatic. The term "layoff" was used, but that was window dressing for a full-scale termination. This was the low point in an otherwise unblemished career.

It was an ordinary workday in November. The administrator for the division came into our work area. He made an occasional appearance, so I thought nothing of it until he asked me to follow him to one of the back cubicles. Since he singled me out, I knew intuitively that something was brewing. The cubicle had a door, but was open otherwise, thus severely limiting any sense of privacy. Upon seating, I was handed a piece of paper and was asked to read it. The words "layoff" and "termination" and "downsizing" leaped off the page. I asked him directly if I was being fired, and he gave me an affirmative nod. He requested that I remove the lab coat I was wearing, as it was company property, and return it with my ID. He then asked me to proceed to the Human Resources Department, a five-block walk from the main hospital, to discuss my severance package. Overwhelmed by anger and outrage, I made the decision to remain mute. I wanted to exit with my dignity intact. I retrieved my belongings and left immediately.

Outside the building, I called a friend and told her the news. She comforted me with understanding and support, as she had been through a similar circumstance. After ending my conversation, I stood there, and a surge of fear and uncertainty began. That surge would continue intermittently for many months. I had to concentrate on crossing the street as I negotiated the mid-morning traffic. My head was spinning. I remember feeling anxious and a bit in shock. I was also a bit numb. The thought occurred to me, "What next?" I told myself, "I am a single, middle-aged woman in her peak earning years, for goodness' sake!" The committee in my head was in session and remained there for many months to come.

None of my coworkers said a word following my dismissal. One told me that they were concerned about their own jobs and fear of reprisal. I never heard from any of them again, except one who retired.

Up until this time, I had a flawless record with glowing recommendations from supervisors in the field. The situation that set this in motion was a competence-based decision. My acting supervisor asked me to administer a medication intravenously without an MD's order because she could not reach the MD via pager or office phone. The voice in my head screamed "Don't do it!!" I knew this was illegal. Guidelines for nursing practice in my state call this "dispensing medications without a license," an extremely serious offense. This privilege is afforded only to MD's and nurse practitioners. I risked losing my license and other severe legal consequences. After I refused, another RN gave the medication. When I later asked her if she was aware that she could lose her license for giving meds without an MD's sanction, she replied, "No." I also found out that the acting supervisor had limited clinical hospital experience, which is crucial when a decision of this type is made.

I had a great deal of clinical experience, including in medical, surgical, and post-open-heart ICU settings. I had been a professional registered nurse for three decades. I enjoyed working with patients and got on well with my coworkers. I had been working at this job for seven years and felt well-versed and comfortable with my responsibilities.

Unbeknownst to me and other staff, the acting supervisor was about to become my boss.

An exodus of four people happened in the next year. Write-ups and petty fault-finding began as soon as she assumed her role as our new supervisor and continued until my "termination." I mentioned one day that I needed new eyeglasses; a week later, she wrote me up for "needing new glasses" because I had written over the line separating two columns on a patient intake form. I was sanctioned for things that my coworkers received a pass for. The inequity was glaring.

I protested the frivolous and unfair nature of these write-ups to my supervisor, my administrator, the vice president of nursing, and Human Resources, but to no avail. I was cavalierly told to transfer out of the department, which was not realistic because of my area of specialization.

Eventually, I realized I had no recourse but to file a formal complaint about this woman's behavior toward me. I hired a labor attorney to fend off a nonvoluntary termination. A termination in my profession can become a permanent blemish on your record, and I was extremely frightened that this would happen. The attorney warned me that this action might provoke a termination. By that time, I was outraged by the way I had been treated and, essentially, abused. I was bound and determined not to let this happen to anyone else, and I wanted this to be precedent setting. It was disheartening to know that rules applied to some and not others. I wanted to do what was right and felt vilified and castigated in the process. I thought, "I'm a child of the Sixties, and we protest what is unjust and blatantly unfair."

I spoke about my situation endlessly with anyone who would listen. I was already in psychotherapy, but now I went twice a week to deal with the overwhelming stress. If I decided to go forward legally, it was explained to me that even being in psychotherapy can be brought up in a deposition. Having been a member of a support group for many years, I sought solace there with the other members, both women and men.

Because I was now in a hostile workplace environment, I decided to proceed and accept the consequences. My lawyer filed a legal document that clearly stated the reasons I believed I was being targeted and provided documented, tangible evidence supporting my assertions. It was filed under the whistleblower laws.

I went to my support group the day I received my walking papers. They had patiently listened to my plight for many months by this time, and when I announced that I had been "laid off," they congratulated me and applauded. It made me laugh, and I knew, basically, from that point forward, I would be okay.

My women friends patiently listened and offered suggestions, while the men just encouraged me to find another job. I read numerous books on scapegoating in the workplace and hostile work environments to bolster my already wobbling self-worth. But after my dismissal, I decided not to move forward with any legal action, due to the expense and the fact that I had lost my income.

As the reality of my situation set in, I lapsed into a situational depression, which was only offset by taking positive actions. I fell into self-pity, despair, anger, rage, and hopelessness. I felt vengeful for years. I was able to air these feelings within the safety of my support group, and eventually was able to laugh my way through my morbid thoughts of revenge.

I took nearly a year off to deal with the emotional baggage that this situation had wrought. I survived on unemployment and my savings. I even entertained the idea of leaving the profession entirely. But eventually I began to consider looking for gainful employment. The problem was that my self-esteem was at rock bottom, and I struggled with feeling like a failure. To minimize that, I took free computer classes at the local public library to upgrade my negligible computer skills. I spoke to a career coach there, too, and received help in putting my resume together. Soon I was ready to hit the pavement.

Going on interviews was painful and frightening at first. I had worked in a specialty area for seven years and lacked a compass as to what was out there for me. I wasn't sure what the next step would be. Once I set my mind to look for a job in earnest, it took just a couple of months to land my present job.

At interviews, I told prospective employers that there had been a downsizing, which was true. I was able to produce a copy of the original layoff letter handed to me that November. The gap in my employment was easily explained, since I was assisting my father with his recovery from open-heart surgery and a myriad of medical issues during that time.

I had legitimate fears that I would be given a bad reference, and those fears were not unfounded. At the very beginning of the job search, I attempted to return to a previous employer. I had left on very good terms and was sure that they would take me back. I am still convinced that, when they contacted my former employer for a reference—that supervisor in particular—I was not recommended. For future jobs, I got smarter and used a former friend/supervisor/coworker as a reference. That worked.

I was extremely concerned that this experience would leave me bitter, and perhaps it has to some degree. I am much more guarded at work and I distrust those in authority, who can abuse their power. I did learn a great deal about office politics and how sometimes there is no sense of fair play in business. I also learned to advocate for myself and what I need.

A personal vendetta is hard to recover from, and I believe this was at the very root of this ordeal. It was never about my performance; it was about my refusing to do something illegal. The experience made me lose faith in the human race for a good, long while. The good thing was, I had smart feet. I missed my patients and my long-standing relationships with them, and I realized how meaningful work had provided me with the structure and socialization I so sorely needed. I refused to let myself give in to the temptation to isolate because I felt so alone at times.

Losing that job was a major loss I had to grieve. The process took me a few years, even with ongoing support. I believe I have moved on successfully and can honestly say that "living well is the best revenge." I wish the players no ill most of the time now. However, I am quite vocal about my opinion of that medical center to anyone seeking employment there.

My story has a happy ending. My current job is one I am much better suited for. I feel respected and valued. I feel heard most of the time and enjoy my work and coworkers immensely. The depression lifted as I became more comfortable at the new job. My confidence returned after having been trampled.

I lost that job under difficult circumstances, but I also realized that my job does not define who I am as a person. In the process, I learned that I am resilient, but most of all, I discovered my voice. I stood up for what I believe. Today I am proud of that and would do it all again.

POSTSCRIPT

Jennifer is still employed in the new nursing job she found and is sought out for her knowledge and expertise.

PRACTICAL TAKEAWAYS

- We are far more than our work; it does not have to define us as people.

- Talk about your feelings, as much and as often as you need to; having a therapist is a wonderful support.

- Find something you enjoy doing—learning a new skill, a hobby—and spend time doing it.

- If you are unsure what your previous employer will say about you to a potential employer, use a close colleague as a reference.

- Legal assistance is not free, but you can often get a free consultation.

Chapter 7

JOYCE: I LOVED MY JOB, AND IT BROKE MY HEART

Joyce, a white woman in her mid-forties, was a mid-level executive who recognized that her relationship with her boss was deteriorating.

I had a job with many responsibilities, but I spent time helping others with their work because I believed in being kind and creating positive energy in a stressful environment.

The location of my job was perfect. I lived close to work and rode my bike as much as possible. Viewing Manhattan from the span of a bridge on a bicycle as part of my regular commute was transcendent. Feeling the rising heat of the sun while heading east, absorbing reflections of the skies and skyscrapers in the metallic river, and greeting glistening stars on clear fall evenings as I headed west were daily reminders of the preciousness of life and earth.

I was fond of people at my workplace. I enjoyed seeing them on a regular, even daily, basis. All were intertwined in the network of work relationships.

On good days, my job reinforced how I felt about myself and who I believed myself to be. Other days, I felt underutilized, undervalued, and underappreciated. Regardless, I believed in the goodness of my boss and that the future held promise.

But I started to notice quiet thoughts that I didn't want to believe. I avoided the insistence of my inner voice whispering that something wasn't working for me. It never dawned on me that I could just up and leave this situation, when my inner voice started insisting I pay attention. I felt like I was lucky to be there, even as I came to feel trapped and disempowered.

Eventually, though, I burst out of the constraints of the job and initiated different and better ways of doing things. I talked with other senior executives about ideas for new projects. I asked my boss for responsibilities I thought were natural extensions of my work.

And then, I no longer fit. After more than ten years of giving it my all, on a Friday afternoon at three thirty, when I went into my boss's office to discuss some improvements, I was suddenly no longer wanted. She told me, "You are not easy...I can't control you," that I wasn't any good at what I was doing, and that I wasn't "productive." And just like that, I was fired.

I still remember the churn of horror, the world spinning, and background noise fading away. I remember how bright the sun was that day. I remember the detail of the carpet in the corner I had to turn on the way back to my office.

In my office, stunned, I called my husband and a trusted colleague. Both were shocked. My husband asked if I was okay to bicycle home. I said yes, but I wasn't entirely confident that I would not crash on my route home.

I couldn't leave immediately because I was deeply embedded in a number of projects. I felt obligated to finish what I'd started and not give my boss any cause to complain about me later. If I dropped everything, I figured she'd use that against me in her network, which overlapped with mine, and I had to find a new job.

The following week, I stayed in my office with the door closed, humiliated, putting things in order to turn them over. I shared the news with people I worked with directly. Someone told me my boss was angry I did that, because *she* wanted to tell them.

It was a hard breakup. I learned that my boss had cultivated an image of herself as "nice." She told people she was my biggest supporter. She told people how difficult the decision was for her and how tired and overworked she was.

It took me a long time to adopt the word "calculating."

I realized she had taken her story of my "lack of productivity" to the highest levels within the department, and they had agreed that I should leave because she no longer wanted to work with me. It remains a humiliating memory to think of myself walking through the halls cheerfully greeting these people, while all that time they had been approving my departure.

I asked to talk with HR to see what I could salvage. Unbeknownst to me, HR called my boss before I arrived, so I was told I had a communication problem with my boss. That was that. She had the power and the firing stood. My final date of employment would be a month after I had completed my outstanding projects, during which time I would work from home. Later I realized this was part of my soon-to-be-former boss's campaign to appear to be a "nice" person—she didn't "make" me leave immediately.

When you break up with your job, stuff has to be returned and retrieved. I gave back the computer. I moved twenty packing boxes of books and files out of my office on a Saturday to avoid upsetting my colleagues. I left behind keepsakes my boss had given me: a picture frame, a jokey gift—I couldn't bear to keep anything because I was so hurt. I didn't want anything from her around me or my children.

Most hurtful were the reassignment of projects and the letters notifying other departments of those changes, all of which she demanded that I write. She started cc'ing *her* boss when asking me to give materials to her, the implication being that I might not do so. I was gravely insulted.

I never saw her after our last encounter, a week after she fired me, when she said she could not understand why I would not admit that I was "not productive."

I pretended everything was fine when my kids were around; I hid the weeping nights and anorexic days. I lost ten pounds. Financially, I was okay, because I quickly secured another position in the same general area, although I wasn't sure it was the right fit. And then it was over, and I left.

I had tangled thoughts and feelings about peers on similar career tracks who continued to work there. Of course I wanted them to succeed, but this sentiment was not felt without regret. Getting together was a mixed experience. I was happy to see them, but there was also this "thing" that had happened, and I was no longer a part of that world. They moved forward in a linear manner and I did not. I considered avoiding them altogether, but that was also painful. As more time passed, I realized that gently falling out of touch was okay.

After I left, I made new friends and rekindled long-lost friendships. A long-ago teacher who is the embodiment of wisdom, compassion, and generosity talked with me when I reached out. She reminded me of many good things in my life and encouraged me to grieve. It took time for me to understand that, when we lose a job, we not only lose the work and income, but we also lose the net of relationships that were once a part of our hopes and dreams.

I sought out a career coach to talk about how to move forward in the work world. It was frightening to reach out to someone I had never met to explain that I had just been fired and didn't know what to do next, but it was the best thing I could have done as an unprepared, emotionally battered job seeker. She, with her kindness and insight, heard and understood what I was saying and helped me work through the fact that I had been fired. She enabled me to understand what had happened and to begin healing. I was able to make meaning from it: it was time for me to move on from that job and follow the person I had become in my work life. Certainly, it was time to have a better boss, or perhaps no boss at all.

A career coach costs money, which is difficult to contemplate when you've just lost or significantly reduced your income. But a good career coach can meet you where you are and help you move from a state of broken dismay to functionality, because you need to be in a better state of mind to look for work. I wanted to work with a coach, not a therapist. I didn't need to work on myself; I needed to figure out what to do next, workwise.

This healing process takes time. The first year after I was fired, many conversations with my coach were spent in tears.

Even though I was working part-time, I felt like a waste, like my work life was over, and I hadn't accomplished anything. The world was moving forward, while I was stuck in place. I felt like I was in the middle of nowhere. I was afraid to use LinkedIn because I felt so vulnerable and exposed. Putting the end date on that job felt like an advertisement of spectacular failure. Many days—well, most days, in all honesty—I wanted to run away and hide. Instead, I showed up for my part-time job and my family, talked with my coach once a week, read William Bridges' *Transitions*, and went to the gym. I rode my bike, put one foot in front of the other, and felt my feelings.

What has stayed with me from *Transitions* is the idea that the external shell of a house is the first to be finished during the building process; the inside takes more time to complete, and this work is invisible from the outside. In my case, it still hurts on the inside. The heaviness of my job loss lingers, but it has lessened with time, a lot of healing, and some important awakenings.

I spent hours trying to understand why I was fired—including identifying things I might have done differently—and eventually realized she had to fire me. She couldn't get rid of me early in my employment because I was doing critical things that allowed her to pursue her own advancement. But after I became less afraid to ask for what I perceived to be appropriate for myself to advance, my requests conflicted with her vision of my role. She wanted one-directional work relationships that benefitted her alone, whereas I wanted a mutual relationship. I didn't understand this dynamic or its inevitable outcome: she used me and then threw me away.

When I question whether I was productive, my inner voice responds that it was astonishing how productive I was, given what I now recognize as a fundamental personality mismatch. Because formal reviews didn't exist, I had no clues along the way about how my boss felt about my performance, nor was there a chance for me to reflect on what I needed from the environment to grow. There was no language or possibility to have this type of formal conversation.

I found some freelance work using various abilities, so was able to end the part-time job. I spend more time with my children, who are mercifully too young to understand how the world of adults can batter their parents and, by extension, their potential well-being in this Western world. Being regularly present with them as they grow up is something I almost missed. In this regard, getting fired opened up a new internal space.

My parents both worked outside the home—my mother fought to do it!—and I thought my life would be career-oriented like hers. Instead, I am learning that being a parent with work who is also at home adds a quiet stability that I did not have before. I love that I can hug my kids throughout the day.

I am not always financially comfortable or confident. It is frightening to be my age without a stable job. Not earning as much has lasting implications for my net worth, my perceptions of my value, and my mortgage applications. I have applied for jobs that I know I am an excellent match for and heard only, "Thanks, but no thanks." Gushing about young achievers is everywhere; ageism is rampant. I stop myself from worrying about what interviewers will think when they see my skin or neck.

I am starting a small business. I am determined to generate enough work that I never again have to rely on one person or place for my livelihood. I am simply unwilling to give anyone that kind of power over my life ever again.

POSTSCRIPT

Joyce is building her small business and freelancing. Joyce has friendly contact with many people from her previous job and avoids her past boss at all costs. She remains deeply wounded by this experience.

PRACTICAL TAKEAWAYS

- It may be difficult to stay in touch with your work friends; this is part of the loss that is grieved.

- HR is not your friend, nor your enemy; the people in HR are there to protect the company and implement your boss's decision to fire you.

- If you begin to feel stifled, undervalued, or unfulfilled, or you want to grow professionally, don't wait! Start looking for a new job!

Chapter 8

RAKA: I HAD NO IDEA THIS WAS COMING

Raka, an Asian American woman in her mid-thirties, was in the Commercial Analytics/Market Research and Forecasting field. She was on maternity leave when she got the Call.

I had the phone in my hand and sat down, I was so surprised.

I had just fed the baby after we returned from the six-week postpartum checkup. On the other end of the line was my manager. He first conveyed that the HR person was with him, and then said something like *We are eliminating your position.*

I had no idea this was coming. When my voice returned, all I could say was, "Why? What happened?"

My emotions were telling me that this was due to performance, but my rational self knew that I had executed and tied up all the projects successfully before I began maternity leave. After fifteen years of experience and being at this company for more than a year, I wanted to make sure that there would be no complications from my absence. I really liked my work, I was learning in my industry, and so I began my maternity leave full of optimism and hopeful that my position would become long-term.

Everything else happened so quickly that I don't remember any exact details other than *We are eliminating your position*. Perhaps there was some intimation about a restructuring. They said they would mail the necessary documents for me to sign, and I remember that stuff being at my door the very next day.

My immediate worry was about health insurance and how I was going to pay for my new baby's vaccinations. I was deep into the process of setting up day care before going back to work in two weeks. My mind raced through all the implications of this sudden information. I was stunned.

I called my husband, who was also completely shocked. We both ended up wondering, *Is this legal?*

He encouraged me to find a lawyer and schedule a consultation. The lawyer said the way a firing is handled depends on the number of people employed by the company. He also noted that the company didn't have to hold on to a position when the incumbent of that position was out for an extended medical leave.

The irony is that I had sought out a small company because I thought it would allow me to have more responsibility, to be more self-directed, and have more "hands on" opportunities. But it turned out that their size meant they didn't have to give me any notice. In other words, they could do whatever they wanted. I was to receive a two-week severance, and that was that.

The delivery of my baby had been complicated, and, after six weeks, I was still extremely uncomfortable and in pain. I had to use a special cushion to sit, and the physical act of walking hurt so much that it was almost unbearable; it required the delicate placement, slowly, of each foot. But I went to the office in person to turn over my signed documents to HR and collect my personal belongings.

One story stays with me to this day. My other child was three at the time and a fan of the movie *Frozen*. We watched it together, and I bought a *Frozen* coffee mug to remind me of our day. I had used the mug at work. I walked into my office and it was on my desk, broken, with a sign on it saying, "Should I replace?" I was stunned by the stupidity and carelessness of that action. And at that moment, it struck me that I was in an unbelievably cold, yes, *frozen* place.

I cleaned out my office in pain. I had to make three trips to the car because I was not allowed to carry heavy boxes. Each trip was slow. I couldn't bend, and I was in excruciating pain. The HR person asked me if I wanted some help and I defiantly said "*No.*" I did not want her help with my things.

The most hurtful aspect of this experience was the sudden shock: it happened only six weeks after giving birth. They did this when I was so vulnerable. Having a job is a big thing. Your first priority in life is your family and then having a job to support your family. They took that away in an instant.

Another hurtful aspect was that there were no answers to help me make sense of it. I asked both the HR person and my manager why, and neither had an answer. I called other colleagues to ask what was going on, and they didn't pick up the phone or return my call. One colleague did answer the phone, but that person didn't know why I had been let go.

There were simply no answers. I was left hanging without anything to help me move forward.

I had seen my husband go through a work experience where he was told he had to let three people from his support team go for no reason. He was horribly upset about it, I cried about it, and we both realized that this behavior in the work world is just not right. Especially as you start to get older and have more experiences and responsibilities that connect you to other people, you start to understand more about life and see how it all connects differently.

It took me two months to get over the trauma of this event. I was going through a lot at the same time: postpartum recovery, needing to find a job, money worries, worries about childcare... It took me a full two months to process it and even begin to think about what to do.

While I was sitting at home with the baby, this was on my mind every day. I kept running everything over in my mind. Was it me? Was it my personality? Was it my performance? Everything felt possible and open to question. What else can you do when you're at home with a newborn? My older daughter went on a cruise with family members, and I thought about going just to escape for a bit, but the baby hadn't been vaccinated yet and reports of Zika virus were just starting to emerge, so I stayed home.

My family was extremely supportive. My husband strongly supported my taking advantage of this time to stay home and take care of the kids. When our first child was born, I was home for four weeks and then went back to work because my husband lost his job due to the Great Recession. So I worked, and he stayed home with our older child. He had the close parenting experience with our first child that I was now having with our second child.

We lived with my in-laws, who were dedicated to eating at home and traditional home remedies, which nurtured our health and our family lives. This environment allowed me to breastfeed and pump extra milk. This was important to me because I didn't produce enough milk for my first child but was able to for this one. I also had space during the day because everyone was at work or school, so even though I ruminated and wondered and questioned and cried, it was okay, although evenings got a little crazy.

By the end of those first two months, I was adjusting to this new norm. I started feeling better and decided that I would find a better job. I stayed home until the baby was six months old and then took steps to get back into the workforce.

I reached out to everyone I used to work with to find another job. I also used LinkedIn, and that is where I found my next job. When I accepted the position, I realized I did not have any residue left over from my previous experience. I didn't tell a lot of people about it during my leave because it was painful, and I wanted to keep this aspect of my life private. However, when I found my new company, they were hiring new employees in full force, so I found my job quickly. I told them openly what had happened to me at my previous job. They were shocked about the way it happened.

I think other women should read the book *The Three Signs of a Miserable Job* by Patrick Lencioni.[14] It helped me realize that, ultimately, you have to manage yourself. As you grow, you become wiser. Working with different kinds of people gives you experience with different personalities, workloads, different experiences, and you gain a feel about it.

Many companies in my area claim they are patient-centric, but I think they also have to be *employee*-centric. They often are not. Part of being employee-centric is having good managers—and ensuring the managers are good. This is important. As an employee, you want to work for someone who wants to help you be successful at what you are doing—a leader who wants to make you a successful leader. These people are so rare. We need more of them, and companies also need to establish these sorts of positive core values for their employees.

In retrospect, I wish I had had the opportunity to express how I felt. As part of being a woman, I was afraid to speak up because I didn't know what the response would be. I asked my boss numerous times to help me prioritize the work that needed to be done, and I just don't think he understood that, by my asking, I was trying to help myself be a successful, strong, and efficient manager. I don't think he had a sense of how to manage a team of people.

I also wish that the company had done a better job of telling me what was going on. I thought I had better relationships with everyone there. If they were restructuring, they should have told everyone at my level. These sorts of things are

---

14   Now titled The Truth About Employee Engagement, Patrick Lencioni, New York: Wiley, 2015.

typically planned well in advance. I wonder now how much of what happened to me was a result of my manager's lack of experience.

At the end of the day, it comes down to what you are passionate about doing and good leadership. You have to have good, experienced leaders lead companies. They have to make rational decisions and think about their employees. They also have to realize that we are not robots. Some of these business cultures don't think about the human mind, they think about what needs to get done today and tomorrow. No one is thinking about long-term sustainability, or the human cost. It's just now-now-now and what needs to happen to overcome the next obstacle. This is short-sighted in all realms. Time is the essence of life and we have to make the most of it.

POSTSCRIPT

Raka decided she will never again sacrifice her personal life for her work life. She is at a new job where this is understood.

PRACTICAL TAKEAWAYS

- Your position can be eliminated when—not because—you are pregnant or on maternity leave.

- It's up to you how and when to tell your story about how you left your last job; for potential employers, craft a story that is both true and neutral.

- Keep track of your own work, goals, and accomplishments, and ask for feedback (you can also manage a bad manager this way).

- We each have to decide on the job-family balance that works for us, despite what our bosses might demand, and for some of us, there may be consequences to this decision.

Chapter 9

LISETTE: I LOST EVERYTHING I EVER DID AT THAT MOMENT

A white woman in her late forties, Lisette was hired to modernize the operations of a demoralized and dysfunctional communications department.

I was hired to reimagine and rebuild a communications department within a larger organization. My boss had gutted the department just prior to my hire, so the remaining staff were traumatized. After I was in my job a few months, even-higher-ups again restructured the department, firing some people and moving others around.

Imagine: a department in shambles, a new person brought in to replace a leader of more than fifteen years, traumatized staff, no one remaining who knew how to organize the next set of goals, and no remaining manager with institutional knowledge. It was a mess.

Then I was given unwanted additional responsibility with no increase in compensation: a second department to manage, housed in a different part of the city.

I have held multiple executive positions in highly complex organizations and developed excellent work relationships.

I believe in being good to people and creating a friendly, respectful work environment because I want people to do well and to like coming to work.

In this position, I inherited a junior-level, millennial staff. I started to hire people and to build teams within my department.

I hired a director, who then hired a person who gave a few of us pause. I voiced my concern about fit, but it was the person she wanted.

My boss was difficult. She often yelled or shouted expletives during our calls and interactions. It upset me, but I tried to stay even and not respond in the moment. In one dark moment, though, I went to HR in tears due to her behavior. The head of HR told me I was being bullied. They told me they could start an investigation, which I rejected.

Soon after, at an executive retreat with other leaders from the organization, I received a tearful call from my staff, saying my boss had physically pushed some of them. One of the organization's higher-ups was at the retreat, so I told him what had happened, and said there was a bully in our ranks. He said he would look into it and I should report this to HR. I did so, and then reported to my staff that HR was going to conduct an investigation.

HR never called anyone to follow up about the pushing incident.

I was later informed by one of the higher-ups that this was a matter of optics. Due to the previous, visible firings, there could be no more staffing changes. I was completely stunned. I had never said anything about wanting this person gone, I just wanted her to be respectful and allow us to do our jobs. When I was asked what I wanted to happen, I could only think of maybe getting my boss coaching. But those in the executive suite didn't believe in coaching.

The pushing incident was never discussed again.

A year later, I was summoned to the HR office to discuss a complaint made against me. I was astonished to learn that HR had been told that I was mean to my team members, that I had created a hostile work environment, had no boundaries, overshared, and expected others to do so as well. Where had this come from?

Shortly before this call to HR, I had had an upsetting interaction with the person who gave us all pause. He was really rude and disrespectful when I tried to explain something, so much so that it looked like something was perhaps mentally off. Other members of my staff had had uncomfortable encounters with him, so I was concerned about him. I went to my boss, who offered to talk to him, but never got back to me about that conversation. Now I learned that my boss told him to go to HR about me.

I suddenly realized that this staff person truly despised me. And my boss did not have my back.

I told HR that they could talk to anyone, which surprised them. I told my team there has been a complaint about me, and they should be honest with HR if called and questioned.

Two weeks later HR wrapped up the investigation, saying they had never seen such a contrast between what they heard in interviews and what was in the complaint. They told me I was deeply loved and respected, and considered thoughtful, deeply caring, and passionate. People said I did what I said I would, that I said what I thought so everyone knew where I stood on issues, and that I fought for my team.

Still, HR recommended that I behave in a cooler fashion, refrain from personal interactions with staff, and that I behave in a less caring way. I was going to get a business partner to help me manage my young team. And I would take a skills assessment test to help the organization help me succeed. This seemed strange to me, as I had figured out how to work with my team and clearly all but one enjoyed working with me.

I apologized to my team for the weeks of interviews and discomfort. I was quivery but kept it together. I told them I would be backing off personally and would no longer attend their life-related events (weddings, etc.). My directors were like, *WTH?* I said I couldn't be perceived as showing any favoritism.

At a meeting with my boss later that day, she told me the higher I went, the more this type of thing would happen. She told me to hire (*expletive*) older people, as millennials were seen as difficult to manage by the higher-ups. The higher-ups were also aware of the investigation's results. They apologized for not giving me a dedicated business partner sooner.

I talked to my proposed business partner by phone and attempted to meet with her in person before she joined my staff meeting. She kept cancelling, then showed up immediately before the meeting, saying she wanted to talk to my staff without me. I thought that was odd but said okay. After I introduced this person, she immediately told me I could leave. This was not the strategy that she had proposed prior to the meeting, but I left as asked.

The meeting ran over time. I could hear things getting loud and heated. When I went back into the room, the looks on the directors' faces were terrible. Bits of what had transpired made their way back to me because people were so uncomfortable, offended, and disgusted by the meeting.

My new business partner had told them that the ground rules of the meeting were that what happened in the room would stay in the room, that you could not refute what anyone else said, and people were to say what they thought about me and our work together. Apparently, the person who complained about me stood on his chair and said *I (expletive) hate that (expletive)* and *I won't be okay until she is fired*. Only a few people monopolized the conversation. It was a character assassination of me. But most people felt they were in the twilight zone.

I asked if anyone had fought back on my behalf. No one had.

That night, I sobbed myself to sleep. I felt betrayed by my team. Why did no one stand up for me? Was it because they were young and inexperienced in the political ways of the work world?

The next day I started packing up my stuff because I wasn't sure I should stay. Then there was a crisis, so we were all working together again.

I tried to meet with my boss and HR about all of this. My boss finally granted me a time slot and asked what I wanted to talk about...*really?!* She said that maybe she'd given me too much too soon. I reminded her that I emphatically had not wanted to run the second department. She said we would talk more the next day.

The next day, I went back to the executive suite at the agreed-upon time. I waited and waited and waited. At last, I was ushered into a room. My boss and the head of HR were there. A piece of paper, a box of tissues, and a glass of water were on the desk.

I knew what this was.

My boss said that they had decided it was time to separate and left the room.

The head of HR took over.

He said it was a generous arrangement; there was COBRA and outplacement services.

I put my head down and started crying. I asked how it was possible that I was the one being asked to go.

Why was that "business partner" allowed to have a meeting like that? He replied that discussing the situation would not be helpful for me.

I said nothing like this had ever happened to me. I had brought only awards and recognition to this department. He said he would step outside and give me a moment to reflect. I composed myself and he returned. I asked him to send the document to me so I could review it with my attorney. He said he had to take my phone and badge and walked me out.

At that moment, everything I ever did was taken away from me.

I had managed to send one of my best friends a note before my phone was taken, so she met me at my apartment. I never went back.

To this day, I have no idea what really went wrong or what my staff were told. I came up with lots of potential stories, but I really don't know. I look back and just don't know what to think. My mom wonders if I share too much of myself with colleagues, but I have a long history of managing people older and younger than myself without any interpersonal problems. None.

Friends were amazed. One friend said, *I told you a year ago to see how long it is until you get fired.* This friend reminded me of the pushing incident and said that you will almost always be the sacrificial lamb when you report a higher-up. My friend loved my integrity but reminded me it comes at a price.

In this situation, my integrity did not serve me.

I called an attorney. I had a ton of documentation. After reading my notes, her first question was *Do you want your job back?* I said *No!*

I had an amazing group of people who came out of the woodwork. People offered me jobs, but I was exhausted. I had enough money saved, so I took the next six months off. I needed time to replenish my soul. I cried a lot during this time.

I started getting calls from recruiters but wasn't interested in any of the jobs. Companies in the same industry reached out, but I was simply too traumatized. I couldn't even update my resume; I was so traumatized.

A friend recommended me for a job. After the interview, I cried all the way home. I remember thinking, *I lost my job. I lost my job.*

I'm a justice-oriented person and am still traumatized. I wasn't perfect and made mistakes, but nothing I did was a firing offense. Not even close. That said, I am no longer afraid of job loss.

Up until that point, I had built my sense of self on my job. So losing my job feels like failure. I still feel emotionally injured, and don't think I can recover fully. Some of my friends think it's taking me too long to heal and ask me why I haven't moved on. I was worried too, until I learned from other women that it can take a long time to recover from this kind of betrayal.

I am trying to view this time as a cosmic gift...like God and the universe are giving me options: the option to slow down, to spend time with my family and regroup. I am currently consulting, and while I prefer being part of a team, I am not in a hurry to take a full-time job. I am taking this time to recalibrate and look forward.

POSTSCRIPT

Lisette is doing consulting work, applying for jobs, and going on interviews. She crafted a true and neutral explanation for what happened, in collaboration with a career coach.

PRACTICAL TAKEAWAYS

- Speaking Truth to Power can get you fired, even if you are in a high-level position.

- The interview process doesn't always reveal what potential employers are really like, so it's not your fault if you don't spot a toxic culture.

- You can't control what people who work for you will say or how they will behave, and they can deeply disappoint you.

Chapter 10

CYNTHIA: I STILL FEEL RAW

After returning from maternity leave, Cynthia, a white nursing administrator in her mid-thirties, found that the work dynamics had shifted quite dramatically.

I still feel raw from losing my job.

I work in healthcare. I live and work in a large metropolitan area where there are many hospitals, but once you specialize, you cross paths with the same people at events like conferences.

One day I was called into the office of a person I had recruited and who had risen to the same level as me. She said, "We aren't doing as well as we thought we would be, and we don't need to have a manager."

I asked what that meant because I was the manager.

At that point, someone from HR walked in and said, "We still find you very valuable and we actually created a very special role just for you."

I was stunned and thought, "How did I get here?"

For that, we have to go back in time. I was recruited to fill a new position at another institute in my healthcare organization. From Day One, it became apparent that this position wasn't thought through. They wanted someone to do what they hired me to do, but they weren't set up for this kind of position. As a result, I always felt like a misfit.

Even so, I was given the opportunity to grow, and I did. I pursued a master's degree because I was inspired by all the opportunity and need that existed in healthcare.

A year into my master's program, I recruited Betty to join our group. Soon she was managing a team. Then, she started taking over programs. And more programs. She didn't manage me, but I noticed that she didn't share information with me or my team, which often led to upset and confusion about what we had to do.

Unexpectedly, I became pregnant. Betty was assigned to help my team during my maternity leave.

From the moment I returned from leave, things went downhill. Betty had, in effect, assumed management of my team and behaved as the *de facto* manager of both her team and mine, which confused me and my team. When I tried to initiate something, she asked accusatory questions like "Why didn't you inform me?" and "What are you doing?"

I brought this to the higher-ups, who thought Betty simply did not understand how to be a manager. I approached her in a professional manner in an attempt to address the situation, but she never relinquished control of anything.

Up until that point, I had been working at a fairly high level. I presented at conferences, appeared on the news, and created programs, and one of my programs had even been described in the *Wall Street Journal*. I had to give it all up.

Suddenly, I was assigned tasks that were the same level as my subordinates. I began to see the writing on the wall.

At one meeting, she attacked me in front of my staff. They were uncomfortable and didn't stick up for me. In part I think it was because there were some cultural differences, and they didn't want to confront a superior.

I remained chatty with everyone else, but not with Betty. I shut down. I second-guessed every single thing I did during the day. She removed me from meetings I was invited to and went herself. She never gave me updates of what happened at meetings. She continued to call staff without me being involved.

I didn't know how to react or what to do. I began eating in my office instead of going to lunch with my staff because I heard she'd made a comment that managers shouldn't eat with their subordinates. I became completely isolated. Betty started calling me out for everything. I was crying at work because there was so much awfulness swirling around.

One day I got called into Betty's office for a meeting. I knew something was coming.

This is where my story began: "We still find you very valuable and we actually created a very special role just for you."

This special job was a bachelor-level position. I had a master's degree. They said my salary wasn't going to change. The only thing that would change for me was that I wouldn't be managing any longer.

Betty said that there wouldn't be a job in her (my) department if I didn't take this job, because my current position was being eliminated.

I asked for time to decide.

My husband suggested that I simply do the job to get paid, but he would support my decision. I talked to my sister and to friends and then to my husband, again and again... Eventually even my husband was upset and emotionally drained from this experience!

Ultimately, I said no thank you, I would not take this job, and gave three weeks' notice.

A week after I gave notice, I went to HR to discuss how I would separate from the institution. Betty was on vacation. Much to my surprise, the HR person said that she had spoken to Betty and today was my last day.

This was a total shocker.

It was already two o'clock. The HR person said to bring in the laptop tomorrow, but I wouldn't have to work. I walked back to my desk. I had suspected this might happen so had been preparing. I had backed up my files, so I wiped my hard drive, took my bag, and said to my coworker, "I'm sorry I can't finish training you because I was just informed today was my last day."

I was really devastated. What had I done to be cast off like this? My staff were upset because I didn't get to say goodbye. I didn't get the usual farewell cake. The only contact I had was the HR lady.

When Betty returned, she wanted to know where the folders for the meeting minutes were. I said if she had wanted to know, she should have been around the day she decided was my last day.

I thought I could recharge, recalibrate, and focus on my resume. I was hopeful that I would find something quickly.

As it turned out, that was hard to do.

In healthcare, it is difficult to find a position in a new company, at least for women, because most professional growth happens internally within your organization. New external hires are rare. There were five hospitals in my area, but few available upper-level positions. And with three kids, I couldn't consider a long, schleppy commute.

I was angry. Really angry.

I believed it was a wrongful termination and that I was targeted because I wanted to do well. My father-in-law is a lawyer. He felt that the mistreatment and emotional damage I suffered was worth additional severance, so he helped me write a letter to tactfully stick it to them and explain how I had been wronged. We asked for additional severance to compensate—and we got it. I collected unemployment, as well.

During this time, I was emotional. I felt like I had to stop talking about my position because people in my circle were over it. I felt maybe I was the problem; I started second-guessing myself and my own abilities and characteristics. I also was angry—*How dare she??!!* I busted my butt at that organization for four years. And after all my hard, devoted work, there was no farewell. I didn't even get a cake! The staff were nervous to be associated with me in any way, and I ended up a pariah.

While job-seeking, I kept myself busy. I chaired a fundraising gala in New York. I purged my basement and spent time with my kids. I have two incredibly supportive sisters, so I would talk and vent to them every day. I would also talk to my supportive husband.

I couldn't get enough of the gossip that filtered back to me, which fed my need to know what kind of drama was going on. Seriously, though, knowing the gossip and the stories helped me see that what had happened to me was not an anomaly. There was a small feeling of victory in knowing that Betty was nuts. But nobody ever told me their feelings about how I was treated. Nobody ever said, "OMG, she is *such* a b****." That validation would have helped me feel better.

I got my license in a nearby state but couldn't find anything. I was getting really nervous. I activated LinkedIn Premium and networked in whatever way I could. My husband networked for me with people he saw in his job.

Eventually, I was recruited to a new, better position. I like this position. I went from one extreme to another: my previous boss wanted to know how long it took me to pee, whereas my current boss is nowhere to be seen. But because I don't see her too often, I know I'm doing good work.

I am confident when I send emails and I know I'm capable, so the second-guessing of myself has ended. However, I am now more reserved than I was. I make sure my emails are professional and have no emotion in them.

Nursing is still mainly a women's field. It seems like women who go up the ladder and are insecure are the most likely to become bullies and intimidators. They create toxic environments. They don't like it if we want to grow. It is different at my current job. My boss is a woman, and she is so secure in her abilities that there is no conflict.

I advise women to save your emails and documentation when things happen. Send them home or keep them on your personal phone—don't rely on keeping them at work. Sometimes people feel bad about leaving a good organization. However, I now realize that the organization really never has your back. They have the organization's back. Always network, always have your resume up to date, and be ready to jump at new opportunities.

I learned that I always have to have my guard up and look out for myself. If I had tried to tolerate the "special" position they "created" for me, the stars wouldn't have aligned for me to be where I am now, which is a better salary in a different environment.

My message to bosses everywhere is to be nice. Being nice goes a long way. I managed okay, but what if Betty had acted this way to someone who then fell into a significant depression, or there was abuse happening at home, or something like that? You never know what is going on in people's lives. My kids still ask me, "Mommy, is your new boss mean like your old boss?" Clearly the kids were aware of my unhappiness. I tell them that I want them to always be kind to people because Mommy's boss was not nice to her, and that was hurtful for Mommy.

I have realized through inspiration accounts on LinkedIn and books such as Dale Carnegie's book *How to Win Friends and Influence People* that it doesn't matter how much success you have; at the end of the day it is your character that matters. I am always trying to strengthen my EQ (a.k.a. emotional intelligence). I am constantly thinking about professionalism—about how to be professional and distant, and what if they don't like me. It's hard not to be liked. It's okay to have emotions, but sometimes you need to have thicker skin.

I don't feel like I have had justice with this situation yet. Yes, I got paid out, I made out, and was able to make it work. However, I am still angry about the way I was treated. Having said that, I do feel strongly that I don't want or need toxic people in my life, so I am continuing to focus on the positive and focus on building my career.

POSTSCRIPT

Cynthia leveraged contacts and got a better position for herself. Then the unexpected happened: her former toxic boss joined her new company. What are the odds? She began buying lottery tickets!

PRACTICAL TAKEAWAYS

- Retaining a lawyer can help you ask for what you think you should get in terms of severance.

- Keep your professionalism intact, whenever possible, especially if your industry is a small one.

- Sometimes new positions just aren't thought through, which can lead to stress between you and your boss regarding expectations.

Chapter 11

CHLOE: I ASKED, "OH, YOU GUYS ARE FIRING ME TODAY?"

As VP for Customer Success, Chloe worked for a tech start-up and then for a software firm in her mid- and late thirties. As a Black woman, she liked that the companies said they were committed to diversity.

The day I was fired the first time, my friend told me, at lunch, that I was going to be fired. My friend didn't have any inside information. She just listened to me talk about how I was being treated by my new boss, the vice president of marketing. Previously, I'd reported to the CEO, one of the two cofounders of the software company where I had worked for three years.

When I got back to the office after lunch, I saw a new appointment on my calendar with my new boss and the vice president of finance. I knew it was happening. I went into the room and pre-empted my boss's speech.

"Oh, you guys are firing me today?" I asked.

My boss started to make the little speech he'd prepared. I asked him to stop talking, because I didn't need the speech.

He told me to grab my jacket and go home, and they would send my personal items later.

I objected. "No, I've been here for three years. I'll go get my own stuff and I'll tell you what to send. And you are not walking me out of here like I'm a criminal. I'm going to say goodbye to people." Which I did, and that felt good.

I was really angry because of the way I'd been treated—more on that in a bit. So, I engaged a lawyer who helped me get a little bit more severance as well as some other little things, like getting them to transfer my office cell phone number to my personal cell phone. They originally refused to do that, as if they owned the phone number. My lawyer succeeded where I did not. They behaved in such a petty manner. But it was par for the course.

I'd been employee number three at this company, hired by a white guy I'd worked with at another company. At the start, it was me, the two white male cofounders, and two other white male software developers. I was doing everything else, including marketing, customer support, and HR, as well as a little software development. Originally, I thought this job was a pit stop, after my prior tech company had been shut down by the woman who ran it. She had been pretty abusive to other women, so I was relieved when she closed the company. I thought of my next job as a place to get some experience, and then move on quickly. Obviously, I stayed a lot longer.

I did well. After a year, I got a promotion and a big raise. I was one of the three people who ran the company. My title was Lead and I was managing a team. I did argue a lot with the CEO, and as I look back, I see that I was immature in some ways.

Things changed when the CEO hired a VP of Marketing, another white man. I'd been doing marketing as part of my responsibilities, so I wasn't happy about this. This new VP cozied up to the white men in the office, especially the CEO and the other cofounder who was the technical lead. He even brought them gifts. There were none for me.

After a while, the CEO decided he was going to "give" me to the VP of Marketing to manage. In a past life, this VP of Marketing had tried to hire me, but I hadn't accepted the offer. He said he didn't remember that, so I reminded him, and said lightheartedly, "Maybe this is our time!" But within two weeks, he fired me.

I'd already talked to the CEO about my issues with that VP, and he said he had the same issues. I didn't trust or respect him (the VP). It became clear to me that the CEO wanted the VP of Marketing to fire me. Someone later told me that the CEO hid during the firing, and when he crept out of the back office in which he was hiding, asked, "Is Chloe gone yet?"

I think the VP of Marketing saw me as a threat because I had also done marketing, and I was in charge of customer success.

Not too long before I was fired, I had lunch with the technical founder—he wasn't my boss, but I'd worked with him the whole time I'd been at the company. We had a long conversation about the company, and, in retrospect, I realize he was actually saying that he was sorry about what was going to happen. He said that we'd had friction over the years, but it was productive friction, we got a lot done. Now I know it was a goodbye conversation and that the decision had been made to fire me a few days earlier. I asked if anything could be done about me reporting to the VP of Marketing. He said there was nothing I could do, that once the VP of Marketing decided on something, you couldn't change his mind. And the tech founder said he wasn't a person to stand up to anyone. So, I was stuck.

After I left the company, I heard that there was an explosion of anger from a lot of staff. The message was "You fire the only woman and person of color; don't you care about diversity?" So, they formed a diversity committee. I don't know what came of that.

Being asked for references by a potential employer is hard because I was at a toxic workplace. I can't send someone to the CEO as a reference for me. So I send potential employers to the tech founder. Every time I do, he gives me a good reference. I think he feels guilty about what happened.

I really lost confidence in myself during that experience. I was out of work for six months, and that was very hard. My identity was bound up in my work. Financially I was okay, as I got four months of severance. But the identity part was tough.

Fortunately, I found a career coach through a friend. Working with her was a confidence boost. We went through my whole life's accomplishments, really looking at them, so I owned them instead of staring back and judging myself. Through that process, I rebranded myself, and that really helped in my job search. I got a job at a firm where it seemed my values meshed with theirs. I had a much better sense of my own worth. And I made more money, which was great.

Again, I managed a team. It's such an honor that people trust me to manage them. That company fired me, and I filed a discrimination claim against them. The company really changed, with the CEO starting to hire people who were diametrically opposed to the stated culture. A sales guy who sexually harassed women. A VP of Engineering who was verbally abusive to me and people on my team, cursing at us. The CEO encouraged what he called "brutal honesty."

I talked to the CEO about these issues, saying, "My gut feels like something bad is happening here." He denied there was anything going on, saying I was imagining things, gaslighting me.

There were overt and covert intimidations of women and people of color. For example, a young Black man who worked on the sales team and was so professional was told by the new sales guy "People don't buy stuff from people like you, they buy things from people like me." That young man knew exactly what that meant, so he put his head down and got another job.

The female cofounder chose to let the male cofounder take power and to be powerless. It was really sad.

A year or so into my tenure there, I was promoted to VP, but the CEO wouldn't give me the compensation that went along with it. Then, after a year, I was told I wasn't acting at the VP level. I said, "I will if you treat me the same, and give me the same comp." I got a little more money. But soon the CEO said the board wanted a VP of Customer Success. That was my title, so I guess they were going to replace me, though he denied that. But he decided to have me report to the head of sales.

I asked how they were going to have a VP report to a VP. He said they would give him the title of Senior VP. It was a demotion, and everyone would know that. The CEO tried to get me to accept that the head of sales would be my boss. He said, "We need you to sell this to your team." I felt like I was being sold from one plantation to another. I had no choice; these white men decided my fate.

During this time, I was working with a coach they paid for, a queer Black woman, and even she got sick of what they were doing. She ended up encouraging me to leave.

The CEO and head of sales used the coaching and my therapy against me, saying things like "Why don't you accept your failure?" He said in writing that I should get my therapist to coach me to be vulnerable around him. I told the new HR person about what he was saying, who thought it was illegal. I think he is a sociopath, and I came to feel physically threatened. Certainly, I felt psychologically threatened.

I knew I had to leave, so I talked to the CEO about working out a package where I left with some severance. He agreed. Then, two days later, he fired me, effective in ten days. Their paperwork said I had resigned, but I hadn't resigned. So, I copied everything potentially illegal and contacted a lawyer. My lawyers were so disgusted by what they heard that they worked on a contingency basis.

They didn't hire anyone to replace me, so it was garbage about the board wanting someone different. When I left, my department was split between Engineering and Sales. Apparently, the VP of Engineering went on an apology tour for breaking the culture, "but it had to be done."

The company said they wanted diverse people, but it was just for face value; they wanted us to be quiet. People in power don't like you to be outspoken, and they bully you so you will leave, and they won't have to fire you. Women began leaving the company, lots of people spoke to my lawyer—women, people of color, LGBTQ people. And people streamed to put negative reviews on Glassdoor. The head of marketing had wanted more reviews on Glassdoor so it happened, just not in the way he imagined.

July 10 was my last day and I had a job offer on July 17, with a better title and more money. This company had contacted me on June 30, but I wasn't planning to respond because I thought I had a verbal agreement with my employer to stay. When they fired me, I contacted the new company and things progressed from there. Actually, I had lots of companies interested in me.

I took a month off before starting the new job. I needed some time to destress. That job took a big toll on me physically. I didn't realize it when I was going through it. It was really toxic.

It was a big relief for me to be gone from that job. My family was relieved. It was clear to my husband that it was abusive. My son hates my old boss, too. He said he'd send this cool toy to my son and he never did send it.

I do still feel fear about that company and that CEO. My new job is located far away, though, so that helps me feel safer.

POSTSCRIPT

So far in her new job, Chloe is not seeing any signs of toxicity or racism/sexism. She and her family are happy living far away from their old location.

PRACTICAL TAKEAWAYS

- You may find that men in charge do not welcome women (of any color!) speaking out. You may get backlash.

- Employers may try to "manage you out of your job" by making your work life so uncomfortable that you choose to leave.

- When no one at the top is willing to be your ally and address conflict related to your position, you probably need to leave.

- Trust your gut. Your gut is almost always correct about what's happening to you.

- It may take time for racism and bias to become apparent, and it's not your fault if you believed it when a company said it valued diversity, equity, and inclusion.

- If you feel you might be being discriminated against, keep copies of every email or other documentation.

- To quickly update your resume, keep a running list of your accomplishments at your job.

Chapter 12

JANE: I WONDERED HOW I WOULD PAY MY BILLS

Jane, a white woman in her mid-fifties, was a recruiter in the aviation industry who prided herself on her exceptional customer service and her knowledge of the industry.

After the 9/11 terrorist attacks, air traffic was severely curtailed. As a result, the commercial aviation company I worked for had to reduce payroll by seven to eight thousand employees. I was advised to take the package they offered. I certainly am glad I did. It gave me benefits that I will have for life. Even so, I still needed to find another job.

I have always been employed and prided myself on exceptional customer service and integrity. After sending out many resumes and going to numerous job fairs, I landed a position in corporate aviation. It was quite different from commercial, but I loved the fact that I was constantly learning. I was finding people jobs and enjoying the people I worked with. I even enjoyed my boss when I first met her. I started going to various industry meetings and was soon involved in and inducted onto various boards in the industry.

Fast-forward two years, and my boss and I were at a convention. On the last day, people were packing up booths early, and I thought I would do the same. I thought I was doing the right thing and helping my boss. She was not there at the time, and when she arrived, she was mortified that I had done that and felt that I should have kept the booth open until the very end. She was furious and claimed that I obviously did not want to be there. She told me I should think of another line of work and she would give me sixty days to continue working, but I would be let go after that.

When we returned, we went to the HR department, and the HR director was in shock. He actually called me back after our meeting, as the boss was in the first meeting, and asked me if I would move to a different department. He thought my departure had nothing to do with my work, but was about a difference in personalities. The department was not to my liking, but it was the only job that was open. The HR director was much smarter than I was, as he knew I would retain my benefits and be able to move into a better position as soon as one opened. I did not know when that would happen, so I decided to leave.

I was annoyed and angry in the beginning, but I felt sharing my emotions would not help anyone. I networked and kept a list of everyone I had contacted. I followed up with them and sent out many, many resumes. All the people I had connected with over the years wanted to help.

One general manager from another company actually became my mentor and cheerleader. He would call each week and ask what I was doing. It became a routine for us. He gave me ideas, motivated me to get out of the house, and made sure I found something.

I certainly went through different emotions in the beginning, and the biggest concern was how I would pay my bills. I collected unemployment for a while, and the former aviation company boss even let me make a placement, as I had found the perfect candidate for one of her openings. She did pay me half the commission. So, life went on.

I did not want to go through my savings and decided I would do temp work. It was way below my educational level, but because the expression says to make lemonade out of lemons, I did so.

I worked for a lawyer as a temp. I worked at a real estate company and had to listen to someone thirty years younger literally teach me to bake cookies (to create an enticing atmosphere at open houses) and how to answer a telephone but not help anyone. That was a short-lived stint, as I came from a very professional, customer-oriented background. I worked at a doctor's office as a receptionist and finally landed a full-time job at a high-end car dealership.

Ironically, when I took the dealership job, I received a call from an HR department where I had interviewed a month before. I really wanted that job and found the person who interviewed me to be smart, eloquent, and really knowledgeable about the business. I wanted to work for her but never heard back in a timely fashion. I made numerous phone calls and sent emails, but no one got back to me.

When I was finally called by HR, I told the individual that I had just made a commitment to start a new position and had to decline going for a second interview with them. It was unfortunate, but timing is everything. It would have been a job with a much higher salary and one that I was excited about. However, I felt that customer service was really important and, if the company could not return a call in an appropriate time frame, I did not want to work for them anyway. Ultimately, that company folded, and the woman I wanted to work for is now a VP at my present company.

I started to work at the dealership. I was paid at a higher hourly rate because of my background. My time was less stressful, and I always met new friends. I continued to network and look for a job back in aviation.

After two years, I received a call from the woman I had placed in my old aviation company, and she told me that my old boss had been fired. Everything comes around, and now it was her turn. I had always kept in touch with the director in HR, and he had me come in for an interview with the new boss. I really liked him, and he hired me. Before I left the car dealership, I purchased a car with an employee discount.

There were others who had left or been terminated by the former boss, and they soon came back. We soon had our old group back, without the person who had poisoned us all. It was a welcome change, and everyone was again happy and productive.

I am still there, but now working part-time. It was my choice, as I felt it was time to smell the roses a bit. My work ethic is the same as when I worked full-time, but now I have a chance to enjoy some things in semi-retirement that I did not have time to do working full-time.

Reflecting back, I feel blessed. Everything does happen for a reason. The experience made me a stronger person. I knew my customer service skills, my education, and my work ethic would get me through many other jobs. When I needed references, I went back to some of the people I worked for during the rough time. They gave me glowing reports and even said they wished I had stayed.

Some people think they will fall apart and be unable to cope if they lose their job, but my experience taught me that you should always do the best job you can. I kept in touch with many colleagues during the difficult times, and they were the ones who advised me to come back as the boss was gone. One should never burn bridges, as they say, because opportunities will open.

I don't wish ill on my former boss. There were things that I did learn from her. That said, when managing people, you need to be kind to everyone. Situations will change and the tables will turn. You never know what will be further down the road.

POSTSCRIPT

Jane retired and began working part-time filling jobs for companies in her industry. She also gives career advice to graduates from her alma mater.

PRACTICAL TAKEAWAYS

- Take the buy-out package when it's first offered! It's the best deal you'll get.

- Kindness is important; your kindness to others will be returned by many people.

- Keep in touch with colleagues from earlier jobs or who left before you lost your job and reach out to them when you are looking for a job; they will often help you.

Chapter 13

ANNE:
I FELT BETRAYED

Anne, a Latina in her late forties, was a beloved Spanish teacher who spent years developing her own curriculum and loved her work.

I was the Spanish teacher for grades K–6 in a local school district, teaching there for sixteen years. When I started, there were no directives regarding Spanish education, so I developed an entire curriculum myself. I enjoyed teaching and interacting with young kids, encouraging them to become aware of different cultures and to appreciate their own culture. I looked forward to going to work every morning and teaching new vocabulary related to different themes.

Our superintendent/principal was replaced. At first, we teachers thought that this would be positive for our district, because our former superintendent was at the end of his career. However, he had been extremely aware of the importance of learning a second language at an early age and had always been supportive of me and my work. He had encouraged me to implement new teaching methods to facilitate second-language learning.

In March, the new superintendent called me into her office, I thought to talk about new teaching ideas for my classes. She started by saying how wonderful it was to expose young children to a new language and what a great teacher I was. But, she went on, this year, the school district budget was in jeopardy and she had to cut some programs. I was taken by complete surprise when she said she was eliminating the entire Spanish language program that I had developed and that she would replace me with a CD program.

I had never before experienced a reaction like the way I felt at that moment.

My entire body froze, my heart started to pump very fast, and tears rolled down my cheeks. First I was numb, and then I felt like cold water had been poured all over my body. I was in shock. I didn't know what to do or say. Multiple thoughts ran through my mind. My oldest son was going to start college at his dream school, we were excited, and we wanted to help him pay for college. And then this happened.

The superintendent told me how she had felt when she was laid off from her prior job and said, "I understand exactly what you're going through." I couldn't believe she was doing the same thing to me.

She went on, saying, "Things happen for a reason."

"I understand."

"Maybe there are better things for you out there."

I looked at her, thinking, "Where are there other things? How are there other things? I haven't applied for a job in sixteen years!" My blood pressure still rises when I talk about it.

I had been in the school for such a long time! I felt so secure, I had tenure, and the community was so supportive of my teaching work that I never thought this could happen.

This layoff had double significance for me because I was working on a master's degree. This was the final year of the practicum phase, and I had to be in a school system shadowing a principal for six hundred hours. I had three hundred hours left to complete.

Walking out of there, I reassured myself. "I have tenure, I have ESL certification, it is impossible for them to knock me out of the system." All the teachers were saying, OMG, OMG, OMG, and were obviously upset. I used to live in the town, I did a lot for it, and so I knew everyone. I knew the members of the Board of Education. I felt betrayed that they had all participated in this decision. This sense of betrayal made the entire thing worse.

I went to the Parent Teacher Organization to ask for help and reviewed all of the activities that I had conducted for the school and community. I also asked why they let the CD language program in. The superintendent found out that I had done this and became extremely nasty in her interactions with me.

I also spoke to the union president at the time, indicated that I was a member in good standing and asked if they could negotiate for me to teach ESL half of the year and English half of the year, so there would be a full-time job with benefits. Nothing came of that, because there was already someone in the ESL job who had been teaching longer than

I had. I realized that I simply had to look for another job because I was not going to get one in this district.

I talked to my husband, my kids, and my friends. I asked everyone for a job, or for help finding a job. I was extremely uncomfortable doing this. I felt like I wasn't stable, and I didn't know who was going to help me. Everyone was nice and supportive, but I didn't know how supportive and nice they would be when it came right down to it.

My next job came through a friend who is connected to an influential person in another school district. It was my last resort, but I called him and asked for his help to get an interview for an opening at the high school. I knew they hadn't called me because they thought I was overqualified but also inexperienced teaching high school students. I just wanted a chance to be considered for the job because I needed to be working at the start of the new school year. My friend came through; I got an interview the day after I called him.

I got the job, but at a much lower pay rate. The school district claimed they did not have more in their budget. So I am employed and I have health benefits, but I make substantially less than at my previous job. I am grateful for the work.

I've come to believe there isn't anything in life that happens without a reason—my reasoning is, "If you can find a positive thing in a situation, then it is for the best." I think I was probably in my previous school district too long. I was not acknowledged there, and I was not where I needed to be. Now, I am appreciated. I have all these students who come to me and we have lunch together and speak Spanish—it is really special. I found an amazing mentor for my master's degree, which I was able to finish. I am also embarking upon a new entrepreneurial activity, and if it goes well, it will be great.

During the transition, I coped as best I could. I powered through the stress. I didn't sleep, and I gained weight—I was almost fourteen pounds heavier by the time I finished my degree. I also went through menopause and suspect it happened earlier than it might have otherwise because of the stress. My older son was away at college and I missed him a lot, and my other son was worrying about taking the SATs. We needed money, so we tried a new financial venture. And even after getting the job at the high school, I had stress because I had to learn everything about the new district and the new job. But I have to say that the high school kids also rescued me—I spend a lot of time with them, and they are enjoyable and fun. I signed up with a nutritionist and now feel a lot better.

This year I am the strongest I can remember ever being. I am not afraid anymore. All the other teachers are worried about tenure, while I see it for what it is: false security. If they are going to get rid of you, they will, so tenure doesn't mean anything really. Besides, I never worked to get tenure; I worked because I loved the work. I view the past positively and am moving on. It's fine when I see teachers from my previous district; we get on together, and things go on as usual. Ultimately, I hope to leave teaching because, although I love it, the pay is just not enough.

Two things got me through this. One was having a family that lifted me up every time I fell. Four times I reached the point where I said I couldn't complete my master's degree. But I talked to my sister, my brother, and my husband, and they would talk me down. As I neared my degree completion, my brother and sister called me every day to see how I was.

The second thing was having faith. And here I mean a faith in yourself, not necessarily a religion. Without such faith, there is not much you can do. My mother used to tell me a Spanish saying: *Recuerda siempre, a mi pequeña, tu fe puede mover montañas, y si puede mover montañas, cualquier cosa en la que puedas creer sucederá.* (Always remember, my little girl, your faith can move mountains, and if it can move mountains, anything you believe in will happen.)

I still really dislike and am angry at the superintendent in my old district. I wish I could feel differently, but I thought she treated me in a discriminatory way. I always felt people in that town discriminated based on one's heritage. It wasn't all of the teachers, but it was enough of them to make a difference. The superintendent was one I felt was discriminatory. When I cleaned out my room after being let go, and this was after I had been there for sixteen years, with files based on research I had conducted and ideas I had developed, and materials I had purchased myself, she made a point of asking whether I was taking my possessions or the district's. I wanted to spit on her for even having that thought.

Where I am now, it's different—I don't feel any discrimination at all.

My dad used to say that I should have been a man—I always was a fighter and fought for what I wanted—I never gave up, and I think that is part of what made it possible for me to continue.

I think women should always have a Plan B ready—even if it's only in the back of your mind. Always be on the alert—nothing is secure in life. Don't think you can say, "Now I'm good, so I can sit and relax."

I wish my leaving had been handled more slowly. I wish that the superintendent had said, "We know you are doing a wonderful job, the budget is a huge problem this year, we are going to cut your hours but make sure you keep insurance because of everything you've done for us. Be ready to close your program in a year." That would have given me time to prepare and to exit. Leaders or administrators should look at the person and what they've done and take that into consideration. I was told in May that my benefits were up in August and I had a kid on the way to college, and this was after years of service to the school and the community. My salary wasn't huge. Frankly, I thought I deserved more respect.

This experience did not change how I identified myself or how I knew myself to be. I am reminded of when my family questioned my choice of the man I married because he made less than some family members, and I told them that money didn't matter to me as much as who he was. Being with a wonderful man was much more important to me than anything else. I always knew who I was and what I am capable of in my decisions. I am moving forward with this knowledge intact.

POSTSCRIPT

Once settled into her new job, Anne's health returned to its former vibrant state. She pursues various entrepreneurial activities outside of the classroom.

PRACTICAL TAKEAWAYS

- Accept that the job is gone. It's over. Let it go.

- You can be fired even if you have tenure.

- Ignore anyone who tells you that being fired "wasn't personal." Nothing could be more personal.

- The stress from job loss takes a physical and emotional toll, so self-care is essential.

- If you ever had (or have) a great boss who supported your work and encouraged you to grow and develop, celebrate and use it as a source of hope for the future.

Chapter 14

BRIDGET: I WAS REALLY GOOD AT WHAT I DID

Bridget, a white woman in her early fifties, was a supervising editor at a publishing company meticulous in her commitment to her work and her work product.

How could they do it? I had worked so hard, some nights until midnight, checking and rechecking each page, making sure that every detail, every fact was perfect. The books would be *so* good and without any errors...but here I was, walking alone on an empty street in a snowstorm, crying, carrying the only thing I wanted them to retrieve from my office before I was escorted from the building: the roses my brothers had sent me for Valentine's Day. I finally made it to my car, carefully placed the roses in their vase on the floor next to me and collapsed into hysterical sobs. I called each of my brothers and said incredulously, "I was just fired." The reply from each of them was the same: "Get home and call as soon as you are there and safe." I did.

The first day after being fired, I slept. The second day, I slept. I slept almost nonstop for what seems like weeks in hindsight. People called, but I didn't want to talk. I just wanted to block out what had happened, especially the events of that horrible day and the way it was handled by my superiors and the Human Resources representative.

Why did they fire me? I have horrible insomnia, and it takes me hours to get to sleep; it is then difficult for me to wake up early in the morning. I was usually at work by nine thirty, but as a supervising editor with people reporting to me, I had been warned by my bosses that I had to be at work by nine. I made adjustments and had been doing fine, but one morning, I overslept and arrived late. My director was furious and called a meeting with Human Resources. I tried to explain my situation, but no one wanted to listen.

I also tried to explain that others in the department had flexible hours, but the reasoning was that, as a supervisor, I didn't have that luxury.

I was out.

I couldn't even go back to my office. My feelings of shock were profound. To add insult to injury, the women who fired me called a meeting of the department and told everyone that they were not to contact me. I learned this from someone who ignored them and called me.

After several weeks, I noticed a glimmer of a different emotion stirring inside me. I was angry. Who in the hell did they think they were to fire *me*? I was really good at what I did, which included final editing of pages before going to print, managing my team of seven editors, *and* meeting with design and production on an almost-daily basis. The schedules were horrific, and there were nights when I didn't leave the building until after midnight so that everything got done. Other people took vacations, but I didn't. No wonder I was exhausted!

I had never had a problem with a boss before, so why now? Why were they so ready to fire a supervising editor who worked her tail off, truly cared for her team and the product they were working on, and had the experience and the knowledge necessary to do the job? My anger grew.

I convinced myself that there must have been something more to my firing than I knew, so I called my lawyer. Now I was hoppin' mad. After I laid out all of the facts and issues, my lawyer told me that there was nothing that could be done, but I felt better that I had at least tried something constructive to release the pent-up emotions and put off dealing with reality: I had not just lost my job; I had been *fired*. They did not want me. I felt that I had been stripped of my identity, my soul.

Okay, now what? I had slept, seen a lawyer, and wandered around my condo in shock for days, weeks. Time became relative. Without daily routines and structure, the days just melded into one another. Prone to depression anyway, I was a candidate for a full-blown depressive episode. I had the good sense to get in touch with my psychiatrist. My brothers were supportive but lived hundreds of miles away. Friends were, for the most part, supportive, but they had their own families and lives.

I began to worry about money. I had no one else to count on for financial support. Where would I get money immediately, other than borrowing from retirement accounts or credit cards? What would I do long-term, especially if I had to tap into my retirement accounts? I got more depressed as I realized how small the publishing world is. Who would ever hire me again? What would happen to my once-pristine reputation, as an editor and manager and as a hard worker and a professional? How would I ever write a resume again? What would I give as the reason for my "leaving" a job after two years?

Each day brought new stresses and new problems to manage. My psychiatrist was a godsend. With his encouragement, I made new contacts, got some freelancing work, and began exercising. Little by little, *very* slowly, the depression, along with the anger, began to abate.

I was fired in April. Through my new contacts, by September, I had a new job as an executive editor—a higher position. I enjoyed being in the workforce again. But whenever I saw people from my former job, I regressed: I was angry, I sulked, I wanted to scream, my confidence was shaken. One of my best friends still worked at the company that had fired me, so I knew I had to do something to make my peace with the situation. I journaled and talked to my psychiatrist, but I still found myself feeling very defensive.

Three years after my firing, the friend whom I had previously worked with had a large party. I knew the women who'd fired me would be there, and I knew I had to go, but I was a nervous wreck. Would they talk to me? Would I *have* to talk to them?

When I first saw them, they were across the room, so I didn't have to even acknowledge them.

Later, however, I thought, *I can't stand this. I am going to talk to them.* I saw one of the women, walked up to her, and said hello. Then, I don't know why or how it came out of my mouth, but I actually acknowledged that I had a role in being fired. I said, "I just want to say that I feel really bad about what happened three years ago. I am sorry if I ever put you in a bad position because of my tardiness. I had a problem with sleep, and I thought I could make it up as long as I worked later and harder than everyone else. You are an excellent editor, you really know how to make good books, and I learned a great deal from you, so I want you to know that I wish you the best." With that, the woman also apologized to me and hugged me. I talked to the other woman, said basically the same thing, and got the same reaction. I learned from a friend that the two women talked about it to colleagues afterward. Later, I had a private chuckle over these events because just months before, the conversations would have been out of the realm of possibility for me. I had finally made some peace with them and the company that had fired me.

Does it still hurt? Sometimes. It's more of a sting than a hurt these days, but I still can't bring myself to tell some people that I was fired. Do I think it hurt my career? I honestly don't know the answer to that, because I'm not sure I would have stayed at that company all this time anyway. Personal issues have led me down other paths, and I am happier with what I am doing now. It is the same type of work, but I do not manage other people, by choice. Instead, I work as an independent businesswoman. I don't make the same money, but I also don't have the same stresses and headaches. I enjoy what I do more—I like having my hands "on the pages" more than worrying about how everything is going to get done.

In many ways, getting fired was much like experiencing a death, and my experience was similar to the five stages of grief that Dr. Elisabeth Kübler-Ross eloquently described in her seminal work, *On Death and Dying*,[15] namely, denial and isolation; anger; bargaining; depression; and acceptance. Even though these stages were complex, interwoven, and nonlinear (as suggested by Kübler-Ross), with many years of hindsight, I can now see my reaction at that time as that of a person who was grieving deeply.

I experienced deep learning and growth, and would say that my greatest personal accomplishment since being fired is learning that it's okay to grieve for our losses and to go through them in stages, back and forth, revisiting each one as necessary. Some things we just don't get over quickly, and that is okay. I have had to grieve a much more profound loss since being fired, and the lessons learned from what happened on that snowy day in February several years ago helped me realize that life processes take time to work through, often a great deal of time.

POSTSCRIPT

Bridget is a consultant who is sought out to solve complex problems and work on high-level projects. She now treats work as "just a job" instead of attaching her self-worth to it.

---

15   Kübler-Ross, Elisabeth, On Death and Dying. New York: Scribner, 1969. Also, Axelrod, Julie. "The Five Stages of Loss and Grief," Psych Central, March 29, 2014 psychcentral.com/lib/the-5-stages-of-loss-and-grief/000617.

PRACTICAL TAKEAWAYS

- There is no formula for the amount of time it takes to heal after a job loss, so allow yourself to "be."

- You can reframe the experience by considering that you are fortunate to no longer work where you were treated so badly.

- We can empower ourselves by owning our part in our previous work situation when we are further along in our healing process.

Chapter 15

CAROL: I WAS "TOO EXPENSIVE" FOR THE ACCOUNT

Carol, an accomplished and highly educated Black woman in her mid-sixties, did all the "right" things to rise within a real estate company.

I was a lawyer and real estate professional who worked for a huge real estate management company, handling the portfolio of one of their major clients. I'd saved the client lots of money, managed complex lease negotiations in their favor, and used my legal experience to ensure that their contracts were buttoned up and protected their interests. I really liked the work, even though the client was difficult.

I hoped to move from that account to another one and had taken many steps to cultivate relationships within the company. I did all the things that executive coaches and successful executives say you're supposed to do to rise in a company. But as a Black woman, it wasn't happening for me. I got noticed, I got meetings, but I basically got nowhere in terms of a new position within the company.

Instead, I got fired.

I had been warned I could be let go, because my current account couldn't afford me—I was the highest paid person on the account. But the person who told me that—someone higher up in the company—also said there would be a period of notice, meaning decent severance. So, I was surprised to get only three weeks' notice. I had expected at least six weeks.

I was surprised the company let me go at all, because I had been put in a management program the year before. I applied for it and was selected. It was a competitive program, and the company is large, so it was an accomplishment to get into this particular program. I finally felt like the company was investing in me and wanted to keep me. I've got two master's degrees and a JD, and I've worked in real estate many years. My application for the program gave the higher-ups their first real look at my background and skills. So I felt positive and as though there might be a chance for me to advance at the company.

After going through this program, I had allies in the company advise me to talk to this person and that person who were high up in the company about possible roles I could have. The higher-ups (all white men) did meet with me and told me the company would find a place for me because they recognized my skill set and education. But nothing came of it. It really depressed me, because it was more of the same old, same old. I was never going to get a role with any power. With my ability and expertise, I could have been in senior leadership and definitely could have owned an account. But not as a Black woman in real estate.

In real estate, the culture is white male "buddy buddy" and this was very much a "traditional" company where all of the leadership was white men. So, I was really dealing with double jeopardy as a Black woman. Black women are treated differently than white women and Black men. In my experience, both white men and Black men can feel very threatened by an intelligent, accomplished Black woman.

I know that my age was also a factor. I was sixty-seven when I was let go, even though I don't look it and I'm always learning more and using the latest technology. I think the kids don't want someone around who's like their parents.

The day it happened, HR scheduled a call with me, so I knew what was coming. The HR person and my manager called me on the phone together. My manager said "I'm so sorry, Carol, but we have to let you go. You're too expensive for the account, and the client keeps pushing to reduce costs." My manager said he was heartbroken to let me go. And then the HR person told me I was getting three weeks' notice and that would be my severance. I was really surprised about the amount of time they were giving me. All those higher-ups who were supposed to be helping me—radio silence. They knew they had screwed me.

I was very angry at first, then I got very sad. My sister was angry on my behalf, which was nice. I talk to her about my feelings and anger at the white male-controlled industry. People at work were pissed for me, the people I got along with and who were rooting for me to get a bigger job there— some women and people of color. I hired a lawyer to try to get more money, but they really dug in their heels and refused to give me any more than the three weeks. They did agree to a mutual non-disparagement clause.

I only told close family and friends about it. I didn't want to tell people in my neighborhood, because it was none of their business and we had pretty superficial relationships. I protect myself from people who don't "get" me, as well as from family members and others who have made it clear they are envious of me and my accomplishments. I figured that out in therapy.

Within a couple of months, I got fired up to find something else. I worked with my career coach to reposition myself to apply for jobs in the nonprofit sector, doing real estate, and I applied for jobs in the real estate sector as well. One company interviewed me for several positions. So far, none have been the right fit, but I felt good about getting interviews.

I really miss the regular paycheck and 401(k) contribution. I'm single and have contributed over time to help support some of my family. I can't do that anymore. My lifestyle has had to change as I cut a lot of costs.

I do like to have a positive attitude. I'm able to read a lot now. I have a nephew who is brilliant and neurotic about being the best. I send him a lot of information about being in the present, enjoying what he is doing right now. I do yoga and see a therapist. I take care of myself—plan my day, reach for healthy alternatives. I'm writing narrative nonfiction. Pre-COVID, I wrote in a couple of coffee shops. During COVID, I write at home.

I can't carry the anger around. I put various people's names in a Bible to be able to let them go. They are miserable people, so I'm really happy to be free of them.

In addition to therapy, I get through the feelings by working with my coach and reaching out to some colleagues and classmates. These are people who know me well, and I can trust their suggestions and advice.

I'm not as desperate as I once was. I have some savings, so I'm okay for now. I'm still accumulating Social Security, but if I don't find something soon, I will probably have to use it. That's where my age comes in—I still have so much to offer, but it's a challenge to get a foot in the door. I am networking, but so many of my connections are with older people. I'm working to connect with younger people who will know more about jobs that are available. In some ways, I want to have my own business. My therapist says I could focus on practicing law and selling high-end real estate.

I was bogged down by all the bureaucracy at my last job, as well as the systemic racism/sexism. It's important for me to call out reality instead of blaming myself for being let go. I'm more highly educated than most of the white men I worked with and yet I wasn't able to progress, despite doing everything right. My white woman coach helped affirm that it wasn't me, it was the system that was stacked against me. I was a pioneer, and I did get far, just not as far as I wanted to get.

I'm glad I have COBRA and that I did get that little bit of severance. One thing I feel good about is that I didn't leave in anger. At least I didn't visibly show them how angry I was.

Leaving in anger may feel cool, but I thought about the consequences and how I was going to live afterward. I might need a reference from my former manager. I want to be able to get that.

POSTSCRIPT

Carol keeps a positive attitude, practices self-care, networks with people of all ages, and continues to look for work. She is working on a big project pro bono with her graduate school and contemplating moving to another city.

PRACTICAL TAKEAWAYS

- You can do everything right, talk to the right people, and still not move forward because of forces outside yourself, including racism, sexism, homophobia, ageism, and the list goes on.

- Protect yourself in your severance agreement with a mutual non-disparagement clause.

- Make sure your professional network consists of people of all ages to make your job search easier.

- Being older in the workforce is frustrating when you're at the top of your game and younger people don't agree.

Chapter 16

MARGRET: I TOLD PEOPLE BEING LAID OFF REALLY MEANS "FIRED"

Margret, a white woman in her mid-forties, was thrilled to take on a new full-time position at a nonprofit, leaving a secure part-time job.

I was "laid off" after just thirteen months in a new job, a job I had been recruited for and for which I left a longtime position at another organization. I took the job to do work that actually made a difference in the lives of young people, and to advance my career: it came with a better title, more money, and more responsibility.

The position was a newly created senior role, overseeing two divisions, one led by a woman who had been with the organization a long time. I was excited because I believed in the vision and mission of the organization, and I was going to be working on issues that I knew well because I'd been working in the field for many years. I looked forward to building good working relationships with my colleagues and figuring out how to add value to the organization's work. My boss told me I was to be a "change agent" helping the organization grow its capacity to take on more complex projects.

From the start, the longtime employee resented reporting to me. She didn't provide me with essential information, refused to come to supervisory meetings, and disagreed with me about any suggestions I made regarding ways to create synergies between the two divisions.

I did develop a rapport with my other report, by complimenting her on her work, introducing her to people who were helpful to her, and securing her some organizational resources. But the long timer never warmed to working with me. It became clear that she did not think this new structure was necessary and was talking to my boss, the founding executive director, behind my back. And the executive director allowed that.

The day I was let go, I had a meeting scheduled with the founding executive director, who was retiring, and the incoming executive director, who had already started. Before I could get into my agenda, they said they needed to talk to me about something else, and I immediately knew that they were going to fire me. They called it a "lay off" because they were "restructuring" due to financial constraints that had led to layoffs earlier. And, in fact, my position was not retained after I left.

I wasn't prepared for that moment. I genuinely thought we were having a work meeting. The tears just started flowing, which I hated myself for. I wanted to appear fine. I didn't want them to know how hurt I was.

I also didn't want them to know how furious I was. I knew there was no point in burning bridges, even though I thought they had treated me very unfairly. So, I kept saying, "It's fine, it's fine, I'll be fine." When I think back on it, I realize it was obvious that I was very upset. My tears told them everything.

I went home for the day, got into bed, and called my husband. I cried to him, but soon it was time to go pick up my son and I had to just get on with it. In a month, I felt resigned to the idea that I was "laid off" and nothing was going to change that.

I felt embarrassed having to tell people. Yes, the organization was struggling financially, but I felt badly about myself. I felt like a failure. I felt that I had done my best, but apparently it wasn't good enough for my boss. I also felt old. Most of my colleagues were millennials, and I thought that made a difference in how they viewed me, as though I was not quite one of them.

People at the organization and external colleagues were sympathetic and felt badly for me, and, while I appreciated that, it also made me feel like more of a loser. It was as though they could see that I had failed to get these women—my two reports and the new executive director—to accept me.

At first, I told people that it was a mutual decision. I think I was attempting to save face by taking some power. But over time, I dropped that charade and told people I was laid off. Then I'd make a self-deprecating remark that of course being laid off really means "fired." But there is really no shame in being let go from what was a no-win situation.

The most hurtful part of the experience for me was that I had left an organization I worked at for over a dozen years where I felt valued. I thought the change would be good for me. But from the get-go, I struggled to find my place there. I was hurt by the way the employees who reported to me didn't want anything getting in the way of how they had always done things. I was also hurt by how the new ED shut me out almost right away. She made it clear that she didn't value me and once yelled at me over a matter where I thought she was really overreacting. I couldn't believe she behaved so unprofessionally.

I started looking for a new job within the same week I was laid off. But I was laid off right before Thanksgiving, so it was an awkward time of year. I updated my resume and gave it to some former colleagues for feedback. No one was that helpful. I started contacting work acquaintances and asking for "informational interviews." It was embarrassing to be looking just a year after starting a new job, and I felt a bit desperate.

What helped the most was getting paid through February of the next year. I think they felt guilty because I wasn't given severance. My end date was the end of February, but I was able to "work from home" for most of it. It was a relief to not go into the office, and to have time to look for another job.

I was very stressed after the end of February when I no longer was getting paid. I coped by meeting people for coffee, going to networking events, and talking fairly regularly with some of my closer former colleagues/friends. My husband was there for me, mainly by being a stable presence. And of course, he was working, so we had that income. Otherwise, my support system consisted of my friends, work colleague-friends, and the internet. I signed up for job alerts and got much more engaged with LinkedIn than ever before.

It felt like it took an eternity to find work. I got my first consulting contract in June. At first, I was only thinking about full-time positions. I stumbled into my first consulting job and then I was open to more. I adjusted more easily than I expected to being a consultant. I've stayed the course as a consultant, although I thought I'd have gotten a full-time job by now.

At any given time, I work with three or four organizations instead. I have mostly conference calls and online meetings instead of in-person meetings. I'm essentially an outsider pushing into each organization instead of an integrated member of the team.

What has helped me get through this time is my determination to work. What hindered me, however, were my insecurities. This experience took a toll on my self-worth that persists. I still don't feel as confident as I once did about trying out new things, challenging myself, and communicating my worth.

In interviews, I sometimes mentioned that I was let go because of financial problems, a half-truth. I think I was underprepared for some interviews because, before all this happened, I had felt relatively confident about my interview skills. But when you're interviewing for a "stretch" job, you have to prepare a lot. I had one interview where I was asked a pretty specific factual question and it was clear from my vague answer that I didn't really know. I also had an interview where I thought I knew the organization well, so didn't scour its website, and missed a new feature of their work that they asked me about. Conversely, after interviewing for a job I didn't get, I asked for and got feedback: I came off as "too prepared" and not spontaneous enough. That was a kick in the pants.

I have always worked, and I care about what I work on. I never doubted that I wanted to keep working in my chosen field. I worry that I'll never find a job where I'm both really happy and really effective in my work, all while being paid an appropriate amount for my years of experience and skill set.

I've ruled out executive director/CEO jobs in the nonprofit world because they entail so much fundraising, which I don't like. I turned down a job offer in part because the ED told me she was looking to hire me as her eventual successor. Also, when you're an ED, the organization has to be your top priority and I can't commit to that. My top priority is my children.

The experience of being fired definitely lingers on.

A close female friend who is not in my field sees it as a blow to my career. Even though she bugs me by bringing this up, she and I also commiserate about facing ageism. Some people who are familiar with the organization that laid me off have made me feel somewhat better because it's known in some corners as an organization that's had difficulty retaining staff.

I recommend to other women in this situation who are unsure about how to handle things, hire a career coach in your field or one close to it. I waited two years to do that and wish I had done it sooner.

This is kind of sad, but don't expect other women in your workplace to be your allies. Find a female colleague-friend with whom you can trade ideas and tips. I have a couple of those folks, and it helps to have someone to reach out to from time to time and who you know will pass possible opportunities on to you when they can.

It's not the end of the world to be laid off, but it's not something you get over quickly, unless perhaps you quickly land another job that you're very happy with.

The most profound change in my life is that I work from home, so I don't commute, and I don't get dressed in work clothes five days a week. I have more flexibility, so I spend more time with my children. I'm less certain about where I'll be in five years. I'm basically taking life more on a day-to-day basis.

I still feel resentful and hurt about my former work. But I know that doesn't help me in any way, so I try to let it go. Even though I'm not sure this is true, I do tend to think there is karma. When you treat someone unfairly, it will someday come back to you.

I run into my former boss and coworkers from time to time. In fact, I'm overlapping with a former colleague on a project right now, and she wasn't directly involved in my situation, so it's basically okay to see her. But when I run into the person who was directly responsible, I'm totally putting on an act of being friendly.

I don't think they should have fired me right before Thanksgiving and the holidays. I think they should have given me a warning and talked with me about what they wanted me to be doing differently. If the finances were so tight that delaying my layoff was impossible, I think they could have offered me a part-time position where I was still getting benefits but could potentially phase out. It's much easier to get a job when you're employed than when you're not.

POSTSCRIPT

Margret still consults but also has part-time employee status at the organization she worked at for thirteen years. Yet, Margret would love a full-time job, so she continues to seek that kind of position.

PRACTICAL TAKEAWAYS

- Doing consulting work is a great way to keep money coming in while you look for a full-time job.

- Laid off really means fired in many cases, which explains why it feels so terrible.

- Don't automatically expect women to be your allies in the workplace.

Chapter 17

PRITI: I KEPT THINKING, "THEY NEVER REALLY LIKED ME"

Priti, a South Asian-American woman in her late thirties, was her household's primary breadwinner when she learned that she might not be kept on at the philanthropic foundation where she worked.

My story of getting fired probably differs from most people's because I got so much advance notice. It came as a total surprise yet has been a painful drawn-out process of leave-taking and personal growth.

I was hired by a philanthropic foundation to work on a specific priority area because of my expertise. I loved working with my grantees and saw that my stewardship of our funding was starting to positively affect the communities and community groups we targeted. I knew from the outset that this was a five-year initiative, and I was coming in at year two. While the board could extend this funding, they could also move to a completely different priority area. Foundations start and stop priority areas pretty frequently.

In March, I gave my boss, who was leaving the foundation, lots of information to present to the board about my area's impact, so they could consider extending the priority area beyond five years. Unfortunately, in June, the board of directors decided to shut down the priority area on schedule, in twenty-one months.

I got the news in an email while waiting for a flight to visit one of my grantees. I immediately wondered whether I had job security or had to begin a job search. Even with that amount of time, I wasn't confident I'd find another job, because philanthropy jobs don't come up very often.

When I returned, I waited for someone to clue me into what the next steps were, but everyone acted as if it were business as usual. I set up a time to speak to the HR director to ask what happens next. She looked confused. I explained that because I hadn't been at this foundation when a priority area shut down, I didn't know the protocol and wanted to understand what would happen to my job. The HR director tipped her head back, as if she were going to laugh. She smiled and told me not to worry because the foundation had transitioned program officers from old to new priority areas. She mentioned some people who had done so, including a colleague of mine.

I told her that I was the primary breadwinner in my household, so I needed to plan accordingly. She told me she wasn't sure about what was going to happen with staffing the next priority area, but that I shouldn't worry. I felt reassured and secure.

A week later, the HR director asked me to stop by her office. When I did, she said, "I don't want you to freak out, and I'm sorry I misled you last week, but we're not sure about what's going to happen with staffing for the next priority area." I realized I should worry.

I said, "To clarify, it looks like, independent of my performance, it's not guaranteed that I'll be working on the next priority area." She said, "Yes, but don't worry." My face got hot, and I remember feeling like I needed to be laser-focused on what I was being told. I was not guaranteed a job. My performance didn't matter. The successful work I'd done with my grant portfolio didn't carry any weight in terms of me continuing to work at the foundation. I wasn't going to be treated like all the past program officers. I was getting scared.

The HR director never brought up the topic of my employment again, nor did I. For seven months, I was in a kind of limbo while working with my grantees. Deep down, I felt like I had no value. I felt like my employer didn't care about me. I felt abandoned, discarded. At times, I felt like a ghost roaming the halls: there, but not really there. My anger and frustration grew, including at myself for not being able to phrase things and advocate for myself in a way that would be acceptable to leadership. I also started to feel isolated as a woman of color in a mainly white environment, especially since my white counterpart didn't get this talk from HR. Her job was secure, while mine was not.

In November, I got a new boss. In December, she did year-end evaluations. I took the opportunity to talk about next year being the beginning of my last year at the foundation.

My new boss was surprised, as she hadn't heard anything about that, and said she'd look into it. A couple of weeks later, she told me she was not sure what my status would be. But she added that I brought this uncertainty on myself by asking about whether I would have a job after the priority area ended. She claimed there was a process for making those decisions, and I should have waited. This was news to me. It was also news to all the other program officers who had transitioned in and out of priority areas without any "process."

In January, my new boss said she should know in a couple of weeks. By the end of March, the only news was that the board would approve a new area in July.

It was destabilizing to not know whether I would continue to have a job. And I was demoralized by their attitude of "Why are you even bothering us about this?" and "It's your own fault for even asking us this question." I got the sense that the foundation's leaders didn't care about staff, or at least not about me.

For the seven months between the board's decision and my evaluation meeting with my new boss, I worked with the same speed and motivation. But by January, my motivation dipped. I felt underappreciated and not valued. I kept thinking, "They never really liked me, this is a good way to get rid of me."

Compounding this was my status as a woman of color. Before my new boss started, I started having problems with an assistant, a white woman. She clearly demonstrated bias against me, including refusing to do work I assigned while happily working for white program officers. In my year-end evaluation, my boss actually blamed me for that situation. I had already talked with HR about this assistant, but they didn't take any action either. I felt even more invisible and not valued.

I decided to start a job search. I couldn't wait for them to make a decision. I started emailing people in my network, especially my foundation network. It was great to have an acceptable reason to leave—the priority area was ending. No one had to know that I was essentially being fired because previously all other program officers had been kept on. I had many coffees and many conversations.

I reconnected with a career coach and talked weekly to deal with a lot of feelings about work and to build a job search strategy. I was angry, sad, *and* strategic. As I processed these feelings, I was able to think more clearly about what I really wanted to do.

I remember one of my conversations with a friend/colleague. She said something that really stuck with me: "You know, you give your time away like candy, so easy and free. It's like you say to people: oh, you want time, okay. Oh, you want time, here you go." It turned on a light switch, and I decided I would now be very clear about where and how I wanted to spend my time.

A colleague gave me a spreadsheet called "What Am I Doing" and I started tracking my activities, time spent, and why I was doing it. I began to say no to speaking engagements that didn't pay me or further my career, turned down an invitation to be an organization's Chair of the Board, and stepped off a board I had led through a huge crisis that wrecked my health. I made space for what was next. When someone I respect asked me to join the board of an organization, I told him how much time I had to give. He said, "We'll take it." Going on that board expanded my network and hopefully will lead to paid work.

During this time, I moved in with my significant other. Initially, I didn't talk to my partner about the job uncertainty because we were discussing what rent we could afford, and I knew I had a job for at least eighteen months. I discussed my feelings about the bias stuff with the assistant with my significant other; it was so overwhelming and traumatizing to experience such overt bias.

People forwarded job postings to me and I started applying. An ally at work encouraged me to apply for a CEO job. I did and was moved along by the search firm. Then the search committee moved me along. While I didn't get that job, I was one of two finalists. More than that, the process was wonderful, because I was true to myself, my whole self.

I developed greater confidence in myself. I went from "Can I be a CEO?" to "I think I can be a CEO" to "Yes, I can be a CEO." For people to see me as a real contender to lead an organization was so affirming for my self-esteem. I had lost so much working at the foundation. I started seeing how all my experiences—including the difficult ones—had prepared me to be the leader of an organization.

The stress took a toll. I was sick for at least one week of every month for several months. I decided to take a vacation and reset. I read a lot of books, including *Transitions* by

William Bridges. That book helped me realize I needed to give myself the space to process the transitions I had gone through in the past year—moving out of my apartment and out of New York City after ten years, the place where I became an adult. Moving to the suburbs with my boyfriend, a Black man, with my Indian parents disapproving...I eased up on my frustration and impatience. I adopted the attitude of "It is what it is."

When I returned from my vacation, COVID had blown up and we were in lockdown. I was so relieved at not having to return to the foundation office. COVID complicated my job search, though. I thought I would have another job by summer. But I'm still interviewing, and it's three months before the priority area will shut down.

If my current employer told me today that they would keep me on, I would accept, while continuing to look for something else. They've shown me how little they care about me, so I would not care if I left them.

As I emotionally separate myself from the foundation, I've become an observer—an outsider looking in. I see that foundation leaders don't really care about grantees. Three weeks into the COVID stay-at-home orders, they had yet to ask grantees what help they needed, much less how to get the help to them. Other foundations built new priority areas overnight to address COVID.

I got clear on what I can and can't fight there. When the president/CEO called me one morning as part of his resolve to check in with each staff person, I knew he wanted to feel good about checking in and not hear about grantees' needs.

163

So I talked about how COVID mirrored the AIDS epidemic and asked about his mother.

Now I'm more likely to choose battles I can potentially win, and principles I must stand up for. But I don't have to be the one suggesting something. I ask my white colleagues to do so, or I phrase an idea as a nonthreatening question. It's not safe to be myself at my workplace. But it doesn't hurt to be more diplomatic and strategic to reach some goals.

POSTSCRIPT

Priti's last day was at the end of her priority area's funding, and she was the only person let go. She had to engage a lawyer to negotiate a nonpunitive separation agreement. Priti works with a coach to cope with the difficult emotions that arise from this experience. She has landed an almost full-time consulting gig that may turn full-time.

PRACTICAL TAKEAWAYS

- You did not cause your employer to treat you badly.

- Read your organization's Employee Handbook (hopefully, they have one) and know the processes for performance review and terminations.

- Working with a career coach can help you cope with the difficult feelings around getting fired; you don't have to manage them alone.

Chapter 18

ALICE: I WAS POWERLESS TO KEEP MY OWN JOB

Alice, a white woman in her early forties, was a program director at a nonprofit who loved helping people in need turn their lives around and expected a lot of herself and her team.

I worked at the same nonprofit organization for thirteen years, first as a staff member working on projects to provide permanent housing for low-income tenants. Eventually I was promoted to director.

I really loved my work. What energized me was 1) winning for people who didn't have power and 2) knowing how to use the system to win with them. For low-income tenants, many of whom were Black and Latinx, there was this small window of opportunity to help them take ownership of their building and manage it. I loved working with them to capitalize on this opportunity and help them take control of their housing from really terrible landlords. I trained them on how to run their buildings.

Over time, because of rising property values, it got harder and harder to help tenants buy their buildings. But my team and I were still putting projects together. That meant a lot to me—we were working together to preserve and protect affordable housing in my city.

I had a good multi-cultural team, I pushed them hard, and I did my best to stand with them and support them. The team included organizers and project managers, as well as architects and lawyers on retainer. I believed that our clients—the tenants—deserved our best. We had to be performing at a top level to be effective.

My old boss left, and another one came in. He and I got along okay—not great, but he pretty much left me alone to manage my team and do the work.

One afternoon, I got a call from HR to come to a meeting. I got nervous because no reason was given. When I got there, I was told by the director of HR, "We're letting you go."

I was totally shocked. She went on to say that I would have until the next morning to clean out my desk. And she gave me a packet of information about severance and outplacement services. I got COBRA, plus unemployment and about six months' severance.

The HR director didn't give me a reason, even though I asked. I was freaked out by being fired. I felt overwhelmed. Yet in the same moment, I recognized that I had done something great and wonderful in my work, that I had helped many people and preserved a lot of affordable housing.

At that point, I knew I would survive being fired. Luckily, I wasn't scared about money because I've always been frugal and always had a stash of money for the proverbial "rainy day."

One thing the organization did that was really helpful was to give me outplacement services with a company that had a physical location. It took strength to walk into outplacement. Once I did, I found that the people there were supportive. I got a lot of help with my resume and job search. Every day, I picked myself up and dusted myself off and got myself to the outplacement location. It was really helpful to have a place to go, and I took advantage of it for six months. Having that support gave me a lot of strength as I was looking for work. I wasn't alone.

Not knowing why I was fired was even more devastating than being fired itself, because it made me doubt my relationships. I wasn't sure what had transpired or what I had done to create such a severe reaction. I couldn't figure out what to change. What didn't I see in myself?

I was overwhelmed. How was I going to pick myself up? Most of my friends were sure I would get another job, as was my partner at the time. I certainly had a lot of connections. But I felt dumb and fat and scared—just as I felt when I was a little girl. I became really reclusive for a while. A part of me just wanted to hide and run away.

Three things made me emerge: Outplacement services, therapy, and my friends. I got support within the outplacement service to figure out how to reposition myself. I went back into therapy with someone I'd worked with since I was a teenager. And my friends were there for me, urging me on because they knew I'd find something. I'd always kept in close contact with a group of women I'd been friends with since I was a teenager and all of us were learning about feminism. So, during that awful, terrifying time, I relied heavily on the rich roots and community of people I'd built over the years from all cultures and backgrounds. I wouldn't have gotten through it without my friends and groups.

It took me almost a year to find another job in another city. The job seemed like the right position, because it was using my skills as a housing organizer. I had good references and a connection who highly recommended me. But it turned out to be not the greatest fit, since the organization was pretty hierarchical, and its founders were outsiders to the city. I am "allergic" to hierarchy, and the residents of the city were deeply suspicious of outsiders "parachuting" into their city. It was difficult for me to overcome the suspicion attached to me as someone employed by the organization, even though I did manage to create some good relationships. Then my mom got sick, and I quit after less than a year to go back home and take care of her.

I took care of my mom and of my best friend who had AIDS. My best friend died first, then my mom. That was a terrible year, it was emotionally draining. Caretaking for my mom took a lot out of me; her Alzheimer's was devastating. And her death and the death of my best friend left a hole in my heart and my life.

I've never fully come back to the work world. I am still broken from being fired and not knowing why. I got jobs, but somehow, they weren't what I wanted to do. I'm pretty independent, so finding a job that fit was difficult.

I did the Landmark program, which was helpful to some degree in empowering me. I stepped out of the work world for a while, and then worked with a career coach who helped me reclaim my skills and abilities.

Honestly, I never came back completely from the experience of being fired. Yes, I had and have friends I can count on, but I wasn't whole. I did feel shame—what had I done that was so bad? I was fancy-schmancy, I had a high-level position—and then I was nothing. That hurt.

I see people from the old organization, and it's been okay; it doesn't hurt that much. Overcoming death is probably the closest equivalent to it. There's still a part of me that wishes they would just say why they fired me. If I messed up, I wish I had a chance to make it right and get closure.

POSTSCRIPT

Alice does volunteer work in community organizing and mentors young people. She also does pro bono consulting on economic development and housing projects.

PRACTICAL TAKEAWAYS

- Outplacement services help. They are there to support and help you, so accept them if they are offered.

- Being suddenly let go can make it hard to find another job in some specialized fields, so give yourself time—it will happen.

Chapter 19

ELAINE:
I FELT INVISIBLE

A white woman in her late thirties, Elaine had been working in public radio at her dream employer for a few years. For the first two years, she'd also had her dream job.

My boss had delayed my performance review for a couple of months. They were supposed to be done by the end of August, then by end of September, and now it was almost Thanksgiving. I noticed on the calendar invite that we'd be meeting in a room different from his fishbowl office—a small side office with no windows.

I don't remember when it started to become clear to me that we were having a conversation about my leaving, rather than what I would do next. At this point, I'd been in my role for two and half years.

My boss and I had met for years informally, with him saying at the end that he was going to hire me someday. Finally, he had a job to offer me. I was ready for my "dream job" working at one of the largest public radio stations in the country with one of the smartest people in the business as his deputy. Actually, it took him another five months to make the job offer. I learned I was pregnant with my second daughter while waiting for the formal offer and I decided to tell my potential boss. He didn't waver in wanting to hire me, eventually putting "Have a baby!" in my fiscal-year goals.

The job wasn't well defined. I was deputy to the head of programming, essentially an executive producer of special projects.

When I arrived in June, the biggest project on my boss's horizon was launching a live morning show that would boldly go up against a nationally syndicated public radio show. It was a huge gamble that leadership felt was urgently needed to attract a more diverse audience to public radio. I went on maternity leave in early August.

When I returned in the fall, I dove into hiring what turned out to be one of the most talented and diverse teams in public radio. We piloted for months and launched in the following April. My oldest daughter was nearly three, and my baby was eight months old.

Now I was deputy executive producer of the morning show. We had a very talented and mercurial (and it turned out also abusive) male host and his cohost, a talented woman of color who struggled in the high-profile role. I worked crazy hours. For more than a year, I went in at three in the morning and often stayed until three in the afternoon. It was my first management job, and I was hiring and scheduling a global staff that worked in three shifts. It was a huge, stressful undertaking, and most days I found it really engaging. In many ways, I felt like I was doing the work I'd always wanted to do. I had good ideas and was part of something *important*.

After a year, I became overwhelmed trying to manage the show and parenting two young children. I had no life other than the show and mothering my kids. Most of the senior folks who'd started the show had already rotated off. Burnout was real.

My boss then hired an executive producer and asked me to leave the morning show to work more closely with him. This put me in murky territory, and I struggled to find my footing in my new role. I was supposed to be a liaison between programming and development, and I picked up odd projects that fell in my boss's lap. I remember telling a friend about six months before I was fired that being at my job felt like sliding off a cliff most days. I said I'd be surprised if I was still at the job in six months, so on some level I knew how bad things were getting.

An important political analysis project came to the station related to midterm elections and I lobbied to serve as the executive producer, hoping the deadlines and clarity of focus would help me stay on track. The project was already late, and I tried to get it back on time. The project ended up being successful in terms of its reach—it was carried on 135 public radio stations—but it was difficult internally. The funder reneged on paying half of the grant, so there were few resources.

So, it was in this context that I ended up in this windowless office near the end of November, with my boss, and the dawning realization that my performance review was sounding like he was showing me the door. He cited projects that had taken longer than he thought they should take and his sense that he couldn't rely on me the way he needed. He said he'd give me the weekend to think about what I wanted to have "happen" next. The windowless office was because he thought I would cry. I wouldn't cry there. When I left the building, I did, of course, cry.

What followed was one of the most historically crappy weekends of my life. I cried a lot. And while I was on the phone with a labor attorney friend, my three-year-old found a bottle of children's Tylenol that she opened and drank twice the dose for her weight. I didn't realize the danger until she became lethargic at a Disney on Ice performance. I called Poison Control and my pediatrician who said go to the emergency room. The ER admitted her to detox her, and I learned a lot about how dangerous Tylenol is. It was terrible.

The next week, I met with my boss and responded to the points he'd raised. I let him know how committed I was to improvement and that I didn't think I deserved to be fired. Just the year before, I'd received an "exceeds expectations" performance review plus a raise. He said he'd take what I'd said, "under advisement" and then avoided me for two weeks. He wouldn't even respond to emails. I felt invisible.

At our last meeting in mid-December, my boss said that my job was over. He became insistent that I had "never been successful" at my job. He felt it was a burden to him that I worried and processed situations verbally. Then he said I'd be paid through the end of January—six weeks away—and it was up to me if I wanted to go into the office.

I went in just one more time, during a snowstorm, to collect some of my personal belongings and files.

He wanted to make it look like it was my decision, but I was so devastated I couldn't play along. I wrote a goodbye email to everybody. On my final day, my boss wrote and asked if I wanted him to arrange a going-away party for me. I said yes, but he didn't do it.

Our babysitter had to stop working because she had hyperemesis gravidarum (extreme pregnancy sickness). Suddenly, I was at home at home with two young kids. Then, a longtime colleague called and asked if I wanted to teach again at the journalism school as an adjunct for my favorite class. This work gave some structure to my days.

I started my journey out from the pit of despair. I cried a lot. For months, I felt like I'd lost my dream job. I had put my boss on a pedestal (a Roman one!) and struggled with the shame of feeling like I had lost his favor. I was devastated because he'd been a mentor to me and taught me so much. I liked him so much.

A colleague suggested I might have to stop liking him so much.

I felt like I had been among my tribe—the smartest, most ethical, and truly funny group of people, all caring deeply about quality journalism—and then I was cast out.

I met several times with the transition coach the station paid for, but I was too angry and too sad to figure out what was next. She suggested I consider project work while my children were so young, so I could structure my hours. That's largely what I did. Once I considered the journalism school as my anchor, I began feeling like things were happening the way they were supposed to.

The journalism school eventually offered me an official part-time job (with benefits!) as the director of the

Audio Program. I loved building that program and took on additional projects to keep my skills sharp, including coproducing an hour-long audio documentary and book with a wonderful colleague.

Reading William Bridges's memoir *The Way of Transition* helped me. I realized I didn't need to rush to the next chapter of my story, and it was okay to be in transition: to keep my eyes and ears open and to try things out. This book helped me be curious rather than fearful.

It helped that my husband was making good money and I loved spending more time with my daughters.

Hard things remain, and I still feel paranoid about failing to this day. I had imposter syndrome at my job—I felt like I was never smart enough. Even when people close to me told me I was in an unwinnable situation, I felt like maybe my self-sabotage did me in. So much so that, one afternoon, my supervisor at the journalism school called me into his office. He wanted to praise me and strategize, but upon notice of a meeting, I thought he was going to fire me.

I was carrying terrible ghosts with me.

It was probably a couple of years before daily self-induced shame wasn't a huge part of my day. This shame is still with me to this day, in ways that hinder my sense of success.

Getting fired made me more sensitive and human. It was like being inducted into a shitty club but finding out there are some pretty cool and talented folks in your club.

I am not grateful for the years of self-doubt and devastation that followed getting fired. It was one of the most heartbreaking things that ever happened to me. While there is part of me that is grateful that nothing worse happened in my life, it breaks my heart to think about how much I loved working there, the mission, the work, and the purpose.

I learned to be more self-compassionate. I made mistakes, but I learned to forgive myself. I wish I'd been more successful at the station, but I also think back to how young my daughters were and how hard everything was at that time. My husband and I were so out of balance. Two examples: at one point, our mail piled up so high that it toppled over almost on our toddler's head. We also forgot to pay our taxes one year. Just totally forgot. We were at that level of being flat-out overwhelmed.

The greatest gift of being fired seems like a cliche, but it's true—I got to spend more time with my family. My daughters were three and five at the time. My flexible schedule allowed me to get involved with their school, and that community helps me grow to this day, particularly around issues of racial justice. I hadn't been the kind of parent I wanted to be, because I'd put work before parenthood.

My boss was a good dad, and I remember when he was firing me that he said I might even be grateful someday. Many years after it happened, I thought I was grateful. If he hadn't fired me, I wouldn't have the relationship with my kids—and likely my husband—that I do today, and those relationships are the most valuable to me.

POSTSCRIPT

Elaine took a full-time job working for a woman she admired greatly, quitting her job at the University's School of Journalism. After two great years at the new job, she is once again looking for work but that's another story.

PRACTICAL TAKEAWAYS

- Forgive yourself for putting your boss on a pedestal and being blinded to their faults.

- Don't fall in love with your job, because your job can't love you back; loving your *work* is different. You can love your work as separate from your job!

- Believe that you are good enough. Don't buy into the "imposter syndrome" that may be plaguing you at this moment: you, and all of us, have been good enough to do many aspects of our jobs.

Chapter 20

UMARA: I DIDN'T WORK MIRACLES

Umara, a Black woman in her mid-thirties, had success over the course of her career in part by calling on other Black leaders, especially women, for their guidance and support.

"We have decided to let you go."

The moment those words were uttered, I remember my vision went blurry for a few seconds. The words tumbled from the voice on the other end of the call: *We have decided to let you go.* As my vision cleared, I turned toward the window. I remember it being a beautiful August afternoon. As the sunlight reinvented the afternoon, all I could say was, *Okay.* My two-year journey as an executive director was over. I was fired.

How I arrived at that moment is a story that began long before that August afternoon. I am a native New Yorker raised in Brooklyn in the 1980s. Like us, my neighbors were mostly Black families with roots in the South or the Caribbean. I had no idea we were poor growing up or that we lived in a bad neighborhood. But I do remember the abandoned buildings and stepping over crack vials. Only when I was older did I understand that, back then, my neighborhood was undesirable. Women my mom called friends were labeled by others as welfare queens. Yet, we thrived. I thrived. My childhood was steeped in a place of love and community.

After college, I knew that I wanted to work in communities similar to where I grew up. At the magnificent age of twenty-two, I had an innocent yearning to do more. This is when my career started in nonprofits. I began in youth development, mostly after-school and summer youth programs. I was lucky enough to have mentors who encouraged me to build relationships with the people I was working with. I remember being told that it doesn't matter how smart you think you are; you don't have the answers. *You never tell someone else what they need in their life.* I was constantly humbled.

Upon finishing graduate school, I decided to focus more intentionally on program development. After years of direct service work, I felt ready to apply my knowledge and experience to program design. I was also taking advantage of professional development opportunities. I was building up my analytical muscle. And I was good. I was creative, patient, and willing to try new things.

I found myself increasingly interested in organizational development and leadership. I was soon managing teams and overseeing large-scale projects. This was an incredible time for me, where I was lost in creativity and learning. I was a consummate student. I also had the incredible privilege of working alongside unbelievable Black people and people of color. Women mostly. I admired their conviction for the work, particularly in naming the legacies and roots of injustice. I spoke in safe spaces about racism, white supremacy, microaggressions. I had a "tribe" of colleagues and women leaders whom I could find solace in with this work. Though they didn't always share their own personal stories of leadership, they were steeped in the mission-based work. Watching them, my confidence in my own leadership grew.

The next step was to become an executive director. I felt ready. For most of my career up to that point, I was hesitant about the ED role. I have always been a "program person" and I did not think I would enjoy a role focused on fundraising. Yet, from a career growth perspective, this role was the right next step for me. My background in direct service, managing teams, and creating programs fueled my confidence in my ability to lead an organization. I also thought that, with the right support, I could learn how to fundraise.

I became a regional executive director for a national organization dedicated to the financial empowerment of low-income families. I already had been at the organization for several years, so I was familiar with its work and the community. My new role came with a lot of excitement and praise:

I was the first Black executive director of that region.

For some, this was an important step in the organization's commitment to diversity. For me, I felt ready to expand the organization's reach to more families.

The only word that comes to mind for my first year is hellish. I entered the role a confident program leader ready to take the next professional step, but I quickly became an overwhelmed mess. I had to learn how to manage an organizational budget, not just a program budget. Rather than simply attending board meetings, I was now leading them. I had new relationships with board members and donors. I was now responsible for raising the money to keep the lights on and pay my hard-working staff.

I soon knew that things were going badly, as I saw some serious problems:

1. **Financial instability.** The fundraising strategy depended heavily on an annual event and there was not a strong pipeline of new opportunities. This was both risky and unsustainable.

2. **Disengaged board members.** Several board members were there way too long. Others were committed to the founder—not me. Most board members were not contributing anything, financial or otherwise.

3. **Failing program model.** I had to implement a revised program model that was not suitable to meet the everyday needs of struggling, poor people. Not only were we ineffective, we were causing harm.

In the tradition I was raised in, you turn to your "elders" to learn. They take the time to provide guidance. These relationships provide strong foundations of support and trust that you leverage in times of crisis and challenge. Steeped in this tradition, I desperately wanted to leverage my relationships with my supervisor and my board chair to help me problem-solve. Unbeknownst to me, my vulnerability cast me as incompetent and unfit for leading in this role.

Now, halfway through my second year, things were getting worse. I had a few fundraising wins, particularly with major donors, but there was yet to be a financial turnaround. I brought on a few new board members and parted ways with others. I felt confident about this new team I was building but heard I had not demonstrated enough impact through the program.

Where I felt the most disappointment in my leadership was regarding the program. I was quickly losing faith in the model, but I was so concerned about demonstrating impact that I did not speak up about the model's flaws. I felt like I was selling something I knew was deficient to a community of people who trusted us. They trusted me. My team distrusted the model, too, but I asked them to work harder to try and demonstrate "success."

Over time, I abandoned my roots and knowledge of my community. I forgot what it was like to have others—outsiders—label people who looked like me and then create a vision that was not in their best interest. I lost my way.

The afternoon when I was fired, I felt like life got sucked out of me. I felt like a failure as a leader.

Some say being fired is like a betrayal. I understand that now. At the end of that summer, however, I did not understand that. What I immediately felt was sheer embarrassment. I was allowed to "control my own narrative," which meant that I could coauthor my resignation details. This carefully controlled narrative meant that I buried my embarrassment and told a story of needing to focus on my family. This was not entirely untrue, but it also was not the truth. Because I was so embarrassed and ashamed, I did not feel like I could tell my own story. I disregarded all of the wisdom I was guided with in trusting in my relationships to support me.

Because when you are fired, you feel an unbelievable amount of shame.

I spent over a year finding the courage to heal and stop feeling like a failure. Part of this process was reconnecting with what I really enjoyed about being an executive director. To my surprise, it was fundraising! I could not have imagined that I would have found such joy in fundraising. I think it was because fundraising was the space where my program background and my experiences growing up in Brooklyn gave me a deeper understanding of the work I was doing. It was because of all these intersections that I became a compelling storyteller and could excite others to want to make an investment in the work. I felt confident in this, and I was good at it; what I needed was more time to build this muscle. Still, I had to come to terms with where I could have done better. Where I did not always speak up or ask for help sooner. This is a huge area of learning that I am leaning into.

There is something else I have been reckoning with: being a Black woman executive director. In recent years, the barriers for Black women in nonprofit leadership[16] have been written about. The further you inch toward the C-suite, the whiter it becomes. As the diversity conversation has amplified in the field, we hear less about work toward equity and inclusion. This is also the case in fundraising.[17]

For a long time, I could not see that, once I stepped into the ED role, I became part of an organizational culture that

---

16   Ofronama Biu, Race to Lead: Women of Color in the Nonprofit Sector, Building Movement Project, February 2019 racetolead.org/women-of-color.

17   Preparing the Next Generation, "Money Power and Race: The Lived Experience of Fundraisers of Color," Cause Effective www.causeeffective.org/preparing-the-next-generation/money-power-and-race.html.

upheld white dominant culture norms. I was focused on getting perfect results and had a dire sense of urgency around everything.[18] I hear this consistently among former executive directors of color.

Because I was so fearful of not being successful and not hitting the mark, I slipped into and upheld these and other norms. I punished myself for taking the time to build relationships and seek out community members as experts. I did not question every time I needed to validate my expertise. I did not hold onto my values rooted in community.

Fast-forward a few years since that August afternoon. I have stopped feeling like a failure. While I continue to learn from that experience, I now have the confidence to know that I am not a failure. I never was. I excelled in some areas in my short tenure as an executive director and was still developing in others. I am reckoning with race and leadership. I have found a group of former executive directors—all Black and women of color—who share similar experiences. We all regret not being able to speak more authentically about the pain we experienced in our time as executive directors. The pain from not speaking up when we needed to. For accepting someone else's vision when we knew the power of our own.

My ancestors and my spirituality continue to guide me in my work. I am now focused more on understanding my purpose and how I want to build relationships with others. Today I am deeply committed to supporting emerging leaders of color. I want to share our stories with young people, who are just as magnificent as I was at twenty-two, who want to do mission-

---

18   "White Supremacy Culture Characteristics," Showing Up for Racial Justice www.showingupforracialjustice.org/white-supremacy-culture-characteristics.html.

based work. I am working on being more vulnerable to share my story. Every day gets easier. With every sunlit afternoon, the shame and embarrassment subside.

POSTSCRIPT

Umara is finding success as a fundraiser after having quickly found a new job through her network of women leaders. Her current employer celebrates consulting with others, group problem-solving, and shared leadership—values that align with Umara's.

PRACTICAL TAKEAWAYS

- Women may be asked to validate ourselves or our experience instead of having our expertise accepted as legitimate.

- When women leaders admit that they don't know everything, many people view it as a weakness instead of a strength.

- Because the path to the C-suite gets more male and whiter at every step, women, especially Black women and other women of color, need to build or access a support system.

Chapter 21

SOFIA: I NO LONGER FEEL LIKE A VICTIM

Sofia, an Italian national in her late twenties, was an organizational development consultant who wanted to remain in the US after attending graduate school here.

When I was fired, the consequences were not simply that I lost my job—I was at risk of losing my entire way of life.

I'd come from Italy four years earlier on a student visa to attend graduate school in California for Applied Psychological Science and Organizational Development. After graduation, I wanted to stay in the United States, but I needed a green card. I looked for a job with a company that would sponsor me to get one. This was challenging, because the employer had to attest that I was more qualified than an American or had unique capabilities.

I finally found a full-time business consulting job at a start-up in Pittsburgh, Pennsylvania, about a week before my student visa expired. They told me they recognized my unique set of qualifications and would sponsor me for a green card. I hated Pittsburgh, but I had to stay because I needed their sponsorship to get my green card.

I was there for about a year, and my green card application was still in process, when I was suddenly let go. They gave me no reason, but I surmised that they ran out of money. I felt terrible about being fired but understood that start-ups often fail, so my anger was somewhat tempered.

What neither I nor they understood was that US Immigration could revoke my green card application because I didn't have a company sponsoring my employment. Now I was truly frightened. When I found out, I moved quickly to find another company. I was willing to do anything because I wanted to stay in the US. Desperation motivated me to talk to everyone I knew. As time passed, I became more and more depressed at the thought of having to go back to Italy and let go of my dreams of living and working in America.

Through friends, at the last hour, I identified a start-up consulting company in San Francisco that did diversity training for Fortune 500 companies. They "hired" me. That meant I would do a lot of free work for them for a year, in return for them sponsoring me to get my green card. From the beginning, it wasn't a great fit. The boss was basically a tyrant and dictator and he took advantage of me from the first day. But to get my green card, it was worth it to me. So I was stunned when they let me go the day before my temporary visa to stay in the US expired.

I couldn't believe the same thing had happened twice. It felt like all I'd done in the US—undergraduate and graduate school—had been for nothing. I had also been betrayed twice, putting my faith in two company owners who did not fulfill their end of the bargain. They took advantage of my need and left me with nothing. Now what was I to do?

When I talked to my immigration lawyer, I learned that I had to leave the next day or I would sabotage any future possibility of returning to the US. I could return later on a tourist visa and begin the green card process again.

I didn't want to lose my chance of living in the US, so I moved very fast. I had to buy an expensive airplane ticket and leave a house full of my belongings. Everything I'd built was gone overnight. It was humbling. I was angry at both employers for not keeping their promise to me. I can see now that perhaps they didn't understand the consequences if they didn't keep their promise, but at the time I was angry and a little despairing.

Thankfully, I had wonderful friends who really came through for me. They boxed up my things and put them in storage. One brought my books and clothes to Italy.

In Italy, I planned my return to the US. I decided to go to New York this time, because the market wasn't very good in San Francisco after the tech bubble crashed in 2000. I had a good friend in New York who I could stay with. I was due to arrive on September 12, 2001.

Obviously, I didn't make it to New York on September 12. The very worst thing was that my dear friend, who worked for Cantor Fitzgerald, was killed on 9/11. Grief and disappointment melded together. It was a very hard time. My family didn't want me to return to the US after 9/11 and the anthrax attacks. They believed it was an unsafe war zone.

I was determined to return to the US, however. I persevered, talking with all my friends and connections to find any kind of job in the US. I ended up getting a job at a brokerage company in Princeton, doing work that wasn't exactly what I wanted to do and making very little money. Plus, I had to commute five hours a day. Initially they did not check my immigration status. However, I did such a good job that they ended up wanting to promote me. Unfortunately, this involved them finally checking my immigration status, and because I didn't have a green card, I lost that job. That was another low point for me. Was I ever going to be able to live and work in the US, a place I had grown to love very much?

Love intervened, thankfully, and I got married to an American citizen. Finally, I got my green card without having to find a work sponsor or do work I didn't like. Being in New York had other benefits for me in terms of career. I made new friends, and one of my new friends ended up changing my life. He introduced me to a global personal development training company. After he told me about the courses, I knew immediately that it was something I wanted to pursue.

I went to my first course and signed up for a very expensive package of courses. It was a huge leap of faith to put it on a credit card. Somehow, I trusted that it would come back to me. I also got a coach, and it soon became obvious to both of us that coaching was my purpose. By the time I met the company's founder, I had coaching experience, and he asked me to help him develop a coaching program and curriculum.

Now I have a full international coaching practice, financial freedom, and a rich, happy life. Everything has turned to gold in my life, while both of the previous companies that fired me without warning are out of business.

When I look back at those two employers, I no longer feel like a victim. Even though I felt like my whole world was falling apart, I kept going. My feelings didn't stop me from taking action toward my goal. Today, I'm actually grateful that it all happened because it led me to personal development. Because those employers let me go, I was free to find my true passion: coaching others to achieve their dreams. I reinvented myself from zero, with help from many wonderful people.

I still have the same coach from all those years ago. My coach has been really important to my continued success. She helped me put together my financial picture and helps me rise above any challenge. I cannot see myself clearly and need a professional to help me work through my feelings and get to another point. There are always solutions—we just need to brainstorm and mastermind to find them.

POSTSCRIPT

Today, Sofia is a coach for entrepreneurs and runs seminars on building businesses. She loves running her own business. Sofia became an American citizen many years ago.

PRACTICAL TAKEAWAYS

- Getting fired is almost always a shock or surprise, so resist the urge to blame yourself for not "seeing it coming."

- Get a coach who has worked with people who have been fired to help you find your new path. Extra points if they've worked with women!

- Maybe not today or tomorrow, but you can empower yourself by shifting your attitude to see possibilities and opportunities.

- We sometimes just have to keep going in the face of complete disappointment, bad timing, loss, and uncertainty.

Chapter 22

ISABEL: I NEEDED TIME AND COURAGE TO TRANSITION

Isabel, a Latina, was a sales and marketing professional who had to dig deep within and reach out to many people for support after losing her job in her late forties. She relied on the same network after a second job loss in her fifties.

I've been laid off twice, and both times it was terrifying to be without work. Even more than that, though, it was frightening to no longer have the identity I had from being part of a company and an industry. Even so, each step brought me closer to doing what I do now, which I truly love.

The first time, I had transitioned into the technology industry. I wanted to work from home because I had two young children at the time. I hired two people who taught me about internet advertising, and I got a job at a new and growing online employment and job listing site. Five months later I was selling advertising to big companies like Bloomberg and Smith Barney. I enjoyed software and developing strategy, wording, and images for internet ads. I came to understand the strategy of the internet when it was in its infancy. I also loved the HR part of the work, strategizing with my clients about writing a great job description and making a job sound exciting so people would want to apply. Essentially, I helped companies market themselves by identifying their purpose, culture, and benefits.

However, the company was sold overnight to another company, and the compensation plan changed drastically. The market took a dive and sales were harder to come by. I was scared to look for work, but I also didn't like what was happening at the company, even though I had been there for four years. Almost the entire original team left, and the company was primarily hiring people under thirty.

My new boss—much younger than me—decided that I could no longer work from home. My territory shifted, and I made half of what I'd made before. There were unrealistic, ridiculous sales quotas to fill. The place became a pressure cooker. I finally told my boss, "This is not what I signed up for!" hoping to negotiate some working-at-home days. With tears in her eyes, my boss said she had to let me go if I didn't come in five days a week. So, I was let go.

Even though I felt like I was done with the job and work conditions, I was unprepared to be unemployed and definitely unprepared to look for work. I didn't know how. I'd never had to look before; people liked me and found me.

I was scared.

Thankfully, I was able to collect unemployment. My husband was self-employed. Unemployment didn't go far because I had to use COBRA for health insurance for me and our daughters. Things were tight, and I started to get desperate.

Because I was desperate, I took a job with a company selling professional employer organization (PEO) services. PEOs provide HR services to other companies. This was a mistake, because I didn't really believe in what they were selling and didn't want to be in that field. The product didn't live up to the promise, so I was uncomfortable doing the kind of hard-sell the company expected. And the work took me out of the digital arena. But I taught customers how to do digital job postings and attract staff. And I made great friends at this job.

That position ended due to restructuring, and I didn't have the time or knowledge for a career change. I had to bring in money and benefits to support my family. Since the easiest thing was to do the same thing, I went into selling internet advertising for an online automotive company. It was good pay and fun for a while but turned out to be the final nail in the coffin for my sales career.

The fun soon evaporated because the car industry included some of the sleaziest people I'd ever encountered. These people were out to get huge discounts, so they'd complain about me or lie about what I'd promised. Usually my boss was on their side. No high-level women worked at the company; it was a man's world. Eventually, I was fired for not meeting quotas. I said, "Thank God!" collected unemployment and didn't feel bad at all. I was relieved to be out of there because it was so unpleasant. Unfortunately, my relief was short-lived.

The year I left the auto sales company was the worst year of my life. This was the first time I experienced truly primal fear. We had enormous medical bills because my daughter became ill and had to be hospitalized. My husband had a heart attack, and his business was going under. We had spent so much money the previous year furthering my other daughter's fencing career so she could get into an Ivy League college that we were in a financial hole. And now I was out of work. We had to stop paying the mortgage.

I knew that I couldn't give up. I had to take things one day at a time, and trust that I would be taken care of. I came to have faith in those things that are unseen. I got down to basics— we still had a roof over our heads and food in our mouths. Friends helped a lot. I walked every day that year with my women friends.

Job hunting was extremely hard. How do you go into a job and do a job interview when you feel like the world is falling apart and you're a piece of dirt? I learned I had the courage to get up and show up. I went into those job interviews and told them everything I could do for them, because I had to. I had the gift of being able to fake it and act as if everything was fine. Meanwhile, I beat myself up for not having a job and worried like crazy.

I knew I could not do sales again. In fact, I turned down sales jobs because my body and spirit couldn't take the pressure.

My transition into marketing began when I joined a small local job seekers group offered for free by two wonderful, kind men with experience in Human Resources and entrepreneurship. One influential exercise was writing down a precise description of three things you did in your life that you thoroughly enjoyed that didn't have to do with work.

My first was painting my Victorian house with historic colors. It was so gratifying to choose wonderful colors and then have people knock on my door to ask about them. I saw other houses painted those colors because my choices inspired them. The second was organizing a dance for a charity event that ended up with many attendees and made a great deal of money. I felt it was really easy to organize committees and people. I don't remember my third, but just writing about those two things made me realize I could do something else. I also saw that my artistic side was not being fulfilled. I thought I would be a color consultant, but after giving it a good try, realized it wasn't going anywhere.

Through friends, I found a coach who helped me realize that marketing could be a good blend of sales and color sense. And marketing has many moving pieces, which appeals to my organizer side. Marketing was a way to use my artistic sensibility, taste, and aesthetics and apply them to branding.

Here's where my PEO sales job became so valuable. Someone I met there went to work at a technology company as chief operating officer. He was a great marketer and salesperson and I kept in touch with a mutual friend of his. I applied to work for him as Marketing Coordinator and got the job. This man gave me the opportunity to make a career transition at age fifty and without a college degree. My fear that my age would preclude my getting work proved unfounded.

I kept working with a coach for my four years at that job. It was a tough place to work and I wasn't valued. I blamed myself for not meeting their expectations. My coach helped me realize that I could learn to value myself even if others did not. I came to understand that I was in a situation not entirely of my own making, and that other people have their own stuff that doesn't reflect on who I am. I saw that people acted out of fear and insecurity and tried to drag me down with them.

After four years, the company went through financial trouble and I was let go—again! But this time, I knew that I was capable. I had learned that I didn't need an MBA to do marketing. So, I looked for another marketing job. My coach helped me revise my resume and made me use LinkedIn. I remember she sat with me as I wrote a LinkedIn message to one of my contacts, telling him what I was looking for and asking for his help. I ended up being hired by that man as Director of Marketing for his company. Finally, I achieved my goal of doing work I loved, and being valued.

Looking back at my journey, I see that I didn't give up during the transition to work I really love. While it was happening, I was scared and didn't have faith in my decision-making. So it was a blessing to find a coach who helped me start to trust myself, and appreciate my talents and abilities. I learned I could trust my instincts—to leave sales, join the job seekers group, work with a career coach, and pursue a new field—marketing. I put one foot in front of the other and did the next right thing. I learned that I could trust the process to reveal more to me. Who knew that a job I hated at the PEO would result in me getting into work I love?

Most importantly, I became willing to let go of my low self-esteem. I worked on a spiritual program to gain confidence in myself. I believe I communicated my lack of belief in myself to other people and made them nervous about trusting me. So, I've done a lot of inside work, coming to believe in myself. I could blame my difficulties on "them" for the rest of my life, but I now know that change happens for the better when I take responsibility for my attitude and actions.

I love my current job. It's challenging and fun and I know I make a difference. I continue to work with the same coach who helps me remain effective and conscious of my own value. Now I read marketing articles and already know most of it, yet I still find ways to learn on the job. I've made a new career for myself at last.

POSTSCRIPT

After several years, Isabel returned to school for a degree in counseling, following her love of helping others. She went through more family and work difficulties before making this decision. Isabel credits her women friends and her faith as key to her ability to continue to have a positive attitude.

PRACTICAL TAKEAWAYS

- Consider joining a job seekers' group to connect with others and get ongoing support and ideas for your job search.

- Look for external causes to blame instead of yourself, because healing cannot start when we are weighed down with self-reproach and shame.

- Spiritual or inner work may lead to a profound transformation, by helping you come to terms with who you were, where you were, and where you want to be.

- Working through difficult emotions—anger, fear, low self-esteem, discontent—is essential so they don't block your change and growth.

Chapter 23

MELANIE: I MOVED FROM CORPORATE CONSTRAINTS TO FREEDOM

Melanie, a white woman in her early fifties, ran a very successful for-profit language school. But she was passed over for a promotion.

I never really noticed layoffs or firing, except for the odd glimpse when I was younger. So I was shocked when it happened to me.

After working in France for many years, I returned to the US eager to get a job in international education administration. I enrolled in a master's program in the field and quickly got a job as center director of a for-profit language school located on the campus of a large private university. I was excited! My district director (DD) believed in me, we worked together well, and I thought that I was finally someplace where I could implement my ideas and programs to help students and staff get the optimal experience out of their studies and their jobs. It seemed to be a place where communication was queen and where people actually liked their boss. This was my dream come true!!

When my DD was promoted, I applied for this position not once, but twice. I suppose I should have known my days were numbered after they said no ever so gently the first time. But I didn't.

The second time I applied for the DD position and did not get it, I was more than demoralized.

The woman who got the job, thereby becoming my DD, made it her personal agenda to get rid of me, probably because I had applied for her job. We had tensions from Day One. I later learned there was an underhanded behind-the-back alliance between the new DD and my academic director (AD) and my AD's assistant to make my life miserable and get me written up. Not knowing this, I told my AD everything, and of course she reported back to the new DD. The DD gave me spectacular performance reviews and told me that she really "loved" me and that I would "go far." However, there was always one little problem that I couldn't fix. And she made life difficult for my teachers; eventually, the DD purged the center of anyone who was loyal to me.

With dismay, I realized it was France all over again, with the attitude of "You can't possibly get 100 percent on this essay, only God gets 100 and teachers get 90, so you'll get 80!" There was so much negativity, underhandedness, and dishonesty! It was so bad that I even began having dreams that "they" came down to fire me. Until, one day, my nightmare came true.

After years of increased workloads, I took my first vacation in almost six years when my son moved to Alaska and I went with him for three weeks. The moment I left, the AD started to turn the wheels by going over my head to the DD to fire even more people and install staff loyal only to her. I returned to an incredibly negative office dynamic.

The day before my DD was coming for a "general visit," I told my registrar that I knew they were coming for me. She was in disbelief and said it couldn't be! I was correct, though. Technically I wasn't fired, because I had done nothing "wrong." In fact, the center was operating extremely well, with good enrollment and student results. Instead, I was asked to leave, after being recited a list of bull, and was offered a severance package. I believe corporate offered the deal because I didn't accept the political, bureaucratic, and power-seeking culture, nor did I play the corporate game.

I had already resigned myself the day before that I would be leaving—I knew it was time, and I was tired of the constant struggle with my boss and the corporate jungle. I wasn't upset or freaked out, though I was a bit in disbelief at the extent of their dishonesty and lack of ethics and morals. I accepted their offer and understood that I was to be gone at the end of the week. In one of those "funny how the universe works" situations, they had to ask me to stay for two additional weeks to complete important work. Of course, I said yes—it gave me time to grieve and to tie up loose ends.

In the US, one spends an inordinate amount of time in the workplace. I was no exception and did indeed belong to the clan of "workaholics." My job was who I was, and I was committed and loyal. So, the schism with this company was, in essence, a failed relationship.

And it failed despite—or maybe because of—my attempts to communicate and operate with transparency, honesty, and love. As time passed, I began to understand what went wrong. My work style and personality were not a good fit with this corporate environment. I'd had to fight to flourish in a corporate environment, and to keep my job.

I vowed that I would not put myself in such a situation *ever* again.

Because I needed a job, I immediately got my resume in order and avidly began looking for and applying to jobs at universities requiring all the skills that I possessed. I applied from Summit to San Jose, got interviews, and then no offers. Soon I was analyzing everything I did, although I felt that the interviews had gone superbly. I was frustrated and wondering what was wrong with me! Was it my age, was I asking for too much money, was I worth that much money, did my previous employer blacklist me, would no one recommend me? This feeling was underscored by the fact that one of my closest colleagues at the university campus where I worked had not answered any of my attempts to communicate with her. Apparently, the universe was telling me to get on another road, but I couldn't quite hear her yet.

I did want to be released from my exhausting patterns, especially of self-doubt. I explored myself through meditations, Unergi healing sessions, and professional counseling. I needed to find work outside the box, for I realized that I as a person had never really been in it. The alternative paths I found allowed me to zero in on anger issues, relationship issues, self-worth issues, and more.

I found a career coach to help me sort through what I wanted to do next. Through my work with her, I became an active member of LinkedIn and connected with a woman with whom I discussed a partnership expanding her work in the intercultural coaching field. This was a fabulous morale boost because it reassured me that I had the skills necessary to succeed. While this venture did not pan out, it was pivotal to helping me see I could create a new business for myself! Things were moving forward. This was my chance of a lifetime to do what I really wanted to do, and I had no intention of missing the boat!

I began two businesses: a dog walking/boarding business with a friend, and the International Student Company Dot Com. The dog business grew fast, as I got the word out at the local dog park and began to get clients who started word-of-mouth marketing. The International Student Company Dot Com fulfilled my love of working with international students and working in an intercultural environment.

By creating these businesses, I fully accepted that the corporate world is not a planet I can live on. Survival takes far too much energy to get anything worthwhile done. It's like taking six dogs to the dog park. You will be consumed by enforcing obedience; any kind of bonding or creative output is stifled by commands.

Both of my businesses grow and expand, focus and divide, but I am on the same path. The road has seemed long at times, but I understand the process, and I have canvassed and gotten clients, reconnected with people at the university where I was based when working for the language school, and connected with other people at other post-secondary institutions who are interested in working with me. It is like building the networks I built in France and at my US employer. They take time and trust, something not easy to give when one has been burned doing precisely that. There *are* good people out there and communities that are just waiting for hard-working, ethical folks. So, changing *my* perspective, as I so often teach internationals to do, is really the key for me. I have willingly put myself in a position where I choose who I work with. I call the shots and I like it.

It's been a big challenge financially. I care for my mother who has dementia, because I can't afford a caregiver. After unemployment benefits ran out, I faced mounting bills. I had to choose between food and mortgage, and food won. I declared bankruptcy and legally separated myself from my mother's debts. Then I sold the house I grew up in before it went into foreclosure. All of these were really difficult in concept but surprisingly simple to do once I faced the reality that I had to do them. We found an apartment to live in where I could care for my mom. And now I am free of those weights around my neck and beginning my next phase of life and career.

I don't think that this process really could have happened had I not sought out the help of a professional coach. That is one expense that was completely essential (and I got a discount!). I continue to have an interest in working with (not *in*) corporations, as well as in helping universities and colleges improve their treatment of international students through more comprehensive and appropriate support systems. My coach keeps me focused in this sense. At times, I apply to those university jobs that really interest me. I am still not being chosen and I am still asking what's wrong, but I care far less and continue to forge ahead with what I have created.

POSTSCRIPT

Soon after she told her story, Melanie's mother passed away, and Melanie followed her dream of moving to Alaska. She became dean of a local university branch, until that position disappeared with COVID-19. Melanie happily volunteers with a sled dog refuge.

PRACTICAL TAKEAWAYS

- If you are facing difficult circumstances, stay in the now, because right now, in this moment, you are okay.

- Now might be the right time for you to pursue your dream.

- Poor leaders may find pretenses to fire people who threaten them.

- You could take the time after being let go to consider what kind of job and work culture would be the right fit for you.

Chapter 24

JEAN: I WAS FIRED TWICE AND AM MUCH HAPPIER

Jean, a white woman, waitressed in her twenties and then held a number of jobs at universities before settling into a job in the technology field in her late thirties.

The first time I was fired, I was twenty-two years old and working as a waitress in an Italian restaurant in New York City's East Village. I had an allergic reaction to some medication and came out in red spots. I felt that this would not be reassuring to diners at the restaurant, so I called in sick. My roommate was also my coworker and was delighted to pick up my tables and tips.

When I returned to work, the restaurant manager was livid. She called me into her small office. She sat in her wheeled chair, and I sat three feet away from her in a chair with arms. She yelled at me for abandoning my roommate/coworker and being selfish and inconsiderate. I replied that my roommate/coworker was happy to get the money and was about to continue about not wanting diners to think their waitress had a communicable disease, when my boss came flying toward me, clamped her hands on the arms of my chair, and hissed, "Don't speak to me like that in my store! You're fired!"

I shouted, in the grandest cliche manner, "You can't fire me, I quit!"

I left the restaurant and came back a few days later to pick up my last paycheck. My former boss was at the bar when I came in; she ran into her office to hide from me as I got my check from the bartender.

It was a lesson in power. I had more power than I realized. By sticking up for myself, I had frightened a bully.

The second time I was fired, I was in my late thirties and working for an interactive agency. I was still relatively new to the business world. The company had grown quickly, and with growth came sweatshop conditions. I, along with everyone else, regularly worked late or very late hours. One night, I was there the entire night, working on a client project. There was also an entire team there working all night on a sales presentation. One of my bosses, who was with them, came by my office and praised me for being there—at three thirty in the morning! This was the same boss who, after a leadership team retreat, took the men out to a strip club and left the women to go home.

He had begun telling me to make changes in the way I managed projects that seemed overly punitive to me. I wanted time to come up with my own suggestions. I was naïve and didn't understand that discussion was not an option. I needed to make it happen. I had also been told by another company leader that basically, I didn't smile enough, and it felt to them that I was always worried. This caused them to lack confidence in me.

With this as a backdrop, I went on a business trip to Los Angeles. While there, I was speaking on the phone to my boyfriend, and realized something. "I have the bad smell," I said. I knew it was just a matter of time before they canned me.

It didn't happen when I came back from that business trip. They waited until I got back from my vacation in August and told everyone that I was now engaged. The following Monday, I was called into a meeting at ten o'clock with my boss and the man who did HR. My boss said, "We're making a change and eliminating your position." This was a lie. I knew they were replacing me with a new woman who had seemed dismissive of me. And so it happened. She got my restructured job. She would be the hatchet woman I didn't want to be.

Despite my having "the bad smell," I was still stunned. I could only sit and listen as he continued, "We're going to vest your stock options ahead of schedule, and you'll get X weeks of severance."

This was something at least. I'd been at the company full-time only about a year, and the industry standard was two weeks of severance for every year worked. It seemed generous, in fact. I had to sign a standard agreement that I wouldn't sue them in order to get the severance and stock options.

I had been in the middle of something when I was called into the meeting, so when I went back to my office, I wanted to make sure whoever picked up my work had those files on the server. But during the fifteen-minute meeting, they shut off my access to the file server. That was my first experience with this kind of corporate procedure, and it seemed petty and unnecessary to me. Now I see that is just policy, but at the time I was insulted and hurt. I wasn't escorted out of the office, though. I would have been really angry about that!

I was also embarrassed. I'd always been the one to end things with places of employment. How could this happen to me? I was mortified.

I soon got over that. I went from stunned to angry. I was livid about the way I'd been treated, as well as the way my team was treated. It was a sweatshop. I'd worked twelve-hour days regularly. They were going to put my team of project managers into a windowless space with no natural light and no real desks, just counters. I felt it was of a piece with making that team scapegoats for anything that went wrong. I understood that a project manager was ultimately responsible for the project, but it seemed there was absolutely no tolerance for error. Projects are a team effort, and I believed there was no acknowledgment of that. I was too new to the corporate world to understand how to shape the discussion.

When this happened, part of me felt relieved to be rid of the stress. Another part felt a little panicked. I had rent to pay—how was I going to afford it? Like most people, I was mainly living paycheck to paycheck.

I immediately applied for unemployment and went to a brokerage where I set up an account and exercised my stock options. I cleared several thousand dollars, so with unemployment and severance, I had enough to live on for a couple of months. I knew I had to start working very quickly, though. I told everyone I knew that I was available for work.

It never occurred to me that I wouldn't get at least freelance work. I felt I was good at what I did, and in my experience, that translated into work. To help with my job hunt and enable me to do freelance work, I spent some of my small hoard of money on a new computer and a fancy LaserJet printer. I already had internet access.

Very soon, through a former coworker, I was called to do freelance work for an internet start-up. I worked there several weeks, after which they offered me a full-time job. I said no because the hours were insane, and the management chaotic.

I decided I would only take a full-time job if it was a place I liked, and the values were ones I shared. I wanted to work with nice people and have reasonable hours. I wanted to feel respected, that my opinion mattered, that people saw me as a person and not just a cog in the machine who produced things.

Someone else I used to work with called me on a Wednesday in October, saying a friend of hers needed a project manager immediately. I talked with the potential employer the same day. I interviewed with him and then the rest of the company on Thursday. I was offered the job on Friday, and I started on Monday.

It was clear in the interview that these were my people. I told the new employer that I was going to be married and needed flexibility in my hours to finish the planning. I would also be going on a honeymoon. That was fine with them; in fact, they were excited for me. They hired me to work with a tough client on a high-profile project with a tight budget and timeline. The client loved me, and I did great work for them. The company had terrific processes and a great support system for their project managers. I learned so much there and made some good friends.

I think my low-boil anger at the last job helped me to not have so much fear. The money I received did help because it allayed some of my survival fear. I assumed I would find work and banished the thoughts that I wouldn't. I knew that if I let those thoughts linger, they would paralyze me, so I kept only the good, positive thoughts. And even though I'm a terrible networker, I was able to reach out to people.

This was in part because, by the time I was fired, I had worked hard to get to a good place with myself. I learned that my life needed to be on my terms. That job had been on their terms; I'd been at their beck and call. I learned I was responsible for setting my limits. I was in therapy at the time, and my therapist was wonderful. I also had a strong group of friends at church and a pastor who was very encouraging to me. All my friends assured me that I was wonderful and deserved a great job. My family reinforced my sense of self and competence, and said it was my former employer's loss. My fiancé also really helped. He was calm and supportive, and we were busy planning a wedding. He had complete faith in me and shared my view of the entire situation. I liked myself, and I believed strongly that everything would work out well. I no longer believed in disaster.

I learned a lot from this experience. I have good antennae and need to trust them. I don't have to work under those conditions and have succeeded in avoiding them. Appearances count in helping people have confidence in me. I smile more and try to be aware of my naturally sort-of-frowny-face because I do want to communicate confidence and assurance and have people trust me. I say things like "To build on that—" when I disagree with someone. Sometimes, you just have to do what the boss wants, and then you can shape the course of events after you've agreed to do something. I read situations better now, so that I can make suggestions before I get ordered to do something. In addition, I know that sometimes there are simply standard procedures, and things aren't personally directed at me.

Before that job, I'd worked at universities where the stakes were lower. My bosses didn't mandate things, and they expected me to discuss decisions with them and even argue with them. I had gotten away with a lot of sass. For-profit corporations worked differently, and I didn't understand that. My boss wanted to go in a specific direction, and I disagreed with it. So, he fired me and hired someone who agreed with him. I look back and see that I was not well-positioned by my training and experience to manage that situation to my benefit.

The world didn't end when I got fired. In fact, my world got better. I learned what I didn't want and headed toward what I did want.

I am still learning.

POSTSCRIPT

Jean built a career for herself in the digital world, first as a consultant and then on staff at a content company. She still respects her gut instincts.

PRACTICAL TAKEAWAYS

- Have confidence in your ability to find work!

- You can get work that is more aligned with your values and work style.

- We have personal power that we can tap into.

- If you get the feeling you might get fired, get prepared; your intuition is probably correct.

Chapter 25

MINERVA: I TOOK A TIME-OUT AND TRANSFORMED

A Chinese American woman in her mid-forties, Minerva was in the advertising industry in a high-powered job, which took a lot of her time and kept her from her family.

I worked in corporate advertising for nearly twenty-five years. When the US economy took a nosedive, corporate advertising budgets were the first to be slashed—followed by the people who manage them. Thousands of people in advertising and media were being let go each day. My company's headquarters were in New York, with six satellite offices in other large US cities. Three of those had already been closed, and it became apparent that the remaining three satellite offices would have to close to keep the company afloat. I worked in a satellite office.

I knew my days were numbered when they started laying off a few people in each remaining office, so I wasn't surprised when my day came. This is not to say that I wasn't nervous about my future or certain about what I would do next. But by the time I got my official notice, I was ready to face the unknown.

I was exhausted from two years of company-initiated last-ditch efforts to save my office/job and picking up the slack left by previously laid-off colleagues. And I was just plain exhausted from twenty-five years working in the rat race. Even before the economic downturn, I had started to feel that the advertising industry was no longer for me.

Corporate advertising/marketing/sales is a fast-paced, high-pressure industry. In addition to short deadlines with relatively no lead time, it required a lot of entertaining, as well as travel to many cities. Though I had played a part in helping many companies garner bigger sales and profits, I often wondered if I had done anything that actually made the world a better place or if I had helped any one person improve their quality of life. So, unlike many people facing a job loss, I was relieved to be given the opportunity to call a "time-out," reevaluate my choices, and possibly reinvent my life.

The layoff itself was sterile. Because ours was a satellite office, I received an email requesting my presence at a nine o'clock conference call the next day, with my remaining office members and the top management in New York. I knew without a doubt that this was the end.

The next day, we got on the conference call. The president of the company, whom I had gotten to know quite well, said nothing. The HR person went over the legal elements of the layoff. I believe the advertising director said a few words. The whole experience was a factual interchange of information and devoid of any sentiment, despite the fact that each member of my office had worked for the company for ten to forty years.

It was not a pleasant day for anyone involved, and I remember thinking that there are really no words that anyone on either side of the phone could say that would make this event any easier. I decided not to utter a word so the legal details could be quickly exchanged, and we could all just move on with our day and lives.

My office was located above the city's train station. After packing up my boxes and saying goodbye to my colleagues, I remember taking the elevator down to the station's grand staircase and thinking, "This is the last time I'm ever going to do this." It was the first time I felt the weight and emptiness of "endings."

In the early days, I did not think very much about what had just happened, because the layoff occurred days before spring break. My husband, two kids, and I had already booked a ski trip to Tahoe. The trip was certainly not the best timing for us financially, but I believed it was important for us to regroup as a family. And I needed physical distance between myself and everything I knew to be my life at that point. I remember a particularly profound moment when I stood at the top of one of the ski mountains, looked around the entire mountain-scape and felt the gravity of how little my existence was in relation to the expanse of all I could see. At that moment, I knew in my heart that everything would work out—it was just a matter of time.

Back at home, I had our floors refinished, cleaned out ten years of basement clutter, and staged our first garage sale. Looking back, the symbolism is obvious: I was laying down a new path to walk, clearing out the old to make room for the new.

This was also a period of self-evaluation of long-held doubts. As a working mom all of my kids' lives, I had always carried some guilt and wondered if I had short-changed them. My working-mother friends and I had often half-jokingly/half-mortifiedly talked about the effects of leaving our children in the care of nannies or daycare, or just plain not being around for our children's every moment of life. But after several months of being a stay-at-home mom and scrutinizing my kids' every action and thought, I concluded they were just fine.

Not only were my children well-adjusted, social, and doing well in school, but they had received the love and care of many different people who had enriched our lives. My kids had learned languages, did far more interesting things in daycare than I would have attempted with them, and had developed a large friend network before most kids get out of diapers. I rested assured that I could contemplate another career path—guilt-free!

I made the most of being home, chauffeuring my kids to interesting summer day camps, planning a "mom/son week" or "mom/daughter week," where each kid had my full attention for a whole week while the other was at camp, and becoming a classroom mom and enthusiastic soccer mom.

While I took the chance to live a role I was previously unable to, I also realized how much my career had contributed to my identity, my purpose, my support system, my self-esteem. I began to miss not having a goal that challenged my intellect, my ability to problem-solve, my strategic thinking, and my competitive nature. I began to resent my everyday assignments: housework, cooking (a previously passionate hobby), overseeing home projects, and driving the kids back and forth.

I especially missed not being recognized for any accomplishments. I found myself in a world where everything I did was a thankless job. Most of my old work friends couldn't relate to my new life, and my new suburban friends couldn't understand my missing the work world. I didn't fit into any world anymore.

I started spending a lot of time alone and reading. Books of choice included individuals who faced and triumphed over adversity, new age spirituality, autobiographies, and random bestseller fiction and nonfiction books. I had always worked out religiously and now tried yoga, the Dailey Method, and biking in forest preserves. I needed mental stimulation and conversation, so I decided to reach out to people who were entrepreneurs. I met with all kinds of people with all sorts of businesses. I learned how they built their companies, and they shared their lessons. Looking back, I see it was a way to casually shop for a new kind of work.

During this time, I fully addressed all of my physical ailments that had gone undiagnosed or untreated when I worked in a time-starved, stressed-out environment. I saw a chiropractor and acupuncturist two to three times a week, and methodically completed a battery of check-ups and tests.

I filed for unemployment and was required to keep track of my attempts to find work. I had talked with many people, but every week, when I went to fill out my sheet, I was aware that no industry sparked my passion. So I started making lists. Lists of what I liked about my previous industry and previous jobs, the skills I had amassed and wanted to utilize or manifest in my next career, the things missing in my last career, my personality traits, what types of things I enjoyed doing, what kind of people I enjoyed, what kind of atmosphere brought out the best in me...etc. I analyzed my family, my upbringing, my past, and my current relationships. Nothing was left unexamined.

I didn't talk to many people about what I was doing or thinking. I was not insecure or embarrassed about my layoff, and I'm not particularly secretive. But I knew I needed to stay away from people who felt the need to direct my path or shape my opinion of myself. Instead, I delved deep inside myself, listened to my own inner voice, and heard what it had to say. With the exception of my husband, a very close aunt and a few very close friends, I didn't say much to anyone else about what I was searching for.

As I have throughout my life, I reached out to a psychologist when I got stuck or felt frustrated and needed someone to help me reframe or identify the source of my feelings. I also consulted an energy healer who predicted most of what ended up happening to me a few years later. But during our sessions, I remember getting horribly frustrated that she was so sure of my life path while I was not. I was afraid that I would never figure out what I wanted to do next.

The oddest part of my story is that I knew what I wanted to do next but needed time to warm to the idea. I read a book on acupuncture and Chinese medicine and felt a strong desire to learn more. I had a profound feeling that this was what I should do. But that feeling scared me in the beginning.

Logically, it should have. I didn't love college, hadn't majored in science, and I would have to go back to school for a minimum of three years. In my mid-forties, I wondered, *Is it too late to reinvent myself, is this just a crazy idea?* It felt incredibly daunting.

But during my acupuncture treatments, I found myself asking the practitioner lots of questions. Clearly, the passion was there.

It took me two years to finally accept that a career in acupuncture and Oriental medicine was my calling. Looking back, I'm glad I explored all my options and made the most of being home and with my family. So, I am grateful that I had the time to do this. I was also lucky. Though my lost income forced my family to live differently, my husband was gainfully employed, and my severance bought the time I needed to reevaluate my entire life.

I believe that my layoff was one of the greatest things that ever happened to me. When we enter the work world, at twenty-one or twenty-two years old, what do we really know about what will make us happy for the rest of our lives? We often fall into fields, positions, promotions, and companies. Then we do what we have to do to pay for our families, mortgages, and bills, perhaps compromising or suppressing our dreams, natural instincts, and sometimes our self-respect. My layoff gave me the chance to stop time and discover who I had become and what I still wanted to accomplish.

I have no bad feelings toward my former company. They did what they needed to do. I have recently had the desire to reconnect with them, particularly the president and advertising director, as I have come to really appreciate the lessons they taught me.

It is true that you are molded by every experience that leads up to your present moment. I really like who I am today, so I am grateful for everything that has happened.

I completed school in the top percentage of my class and loved every minute of it. When you go back to school because you want to, it is an entirely different experience.

I now have a practice and am building my professional network. Don't be afraid to reinvent yourself!

POSTSCRIPT

After completing her degree in Acupuncture and Oriental Medicine, Minerva decided to focus on dermatology. She is earning a reputation for solving dermatological problems that Western medicine cannot.

PRACTICAL TAKEAWAYS

- Even if you lose your job as part of a group layoff, you may still feel emotional about the loss.

- Consider that perhaps it was time for you to leave your job, even if you didn't think so.

- In quiet moments, listen for whispers of knowing what you want.

Chapter 26

WELL, NOW WHAT?

After being fired, both of us felt alone, bewildered, and rudderless.

We asked ourselves, *Now what?*

Now what were we supposed to do? How were we supposed to cope? Who could we talk to? What was normal? Where could we go and hide? How could we keep going? Would this pain ever end?

Our contributors struggled with the same questions and told us what they did. We didn't find a "How To" or "To Do" list, so based on these stories, we've created one.

Just one minute before you hop over to the list!

Sometimes we need to get another job quickly because we need money: we have to pay the mortgage, a car payment is due, the kids are in college, our parents are in a nursing home, or other life realities. We have to act immediately.

The point of this book is that the emotional component of being fired also has to be attended to and managed...gently and with care. Being fired is a difficult life event.

Now, on to the list!

IN THE IMMEDIATE AFTERMATH

Emotional Well-Being

You have just endured a traumatic experience.

In those first seconds, minutes, hours, and days after losing your job, you may feel too stunned to do much of anything. Wrap a metaphorical cashmere blanket around yourself, because shock is normal and to be expected. Give yourself permission to just exist for a bit.

- Be kind to yourself—you're in shock and need extra TLC.

- Avoid people who tell you to "buck up" or otherwise negate how you are feeling.

- "Go where it's warm"—tell your support system ASAP.

- Remember what you do well; *you still do these things well.*

- Take care of yourself: eat and sleep. Walk if you can. Get outside. Seek nature.

- Cry. Sob. Weep. Rage. Feel sorry for yourself. It's okay. By expressing these feelings to safe people, you will help yourself move through them.

- Veg out and stop your brain from ruminating (for example, watch TV, stream a show, listen to music).

- Write or journal about your experience, feelings, thoughts—get it out.

- Remember a line from the poem "Desiderata" that one of us was given by another woman who understood: *You are a child of the universe no less than the trees and the stars; you have a right to be here.*

Practical Well-Being

These are difficult things to do. Even so, you must address these practical steps immediately for your future well-being.

- *File for unemployment as soon as possible.* This is your right, and it will take some time to get activated.

- *Go to your local Equal Employment Opportunity Commission office if you believe you have been discriminated against* because of race, color, religion, sex (including pregnancy, sexual orientation, or gender identity), national origin, age (forty or older), disability, genetic information (including family medical history), or retaliation— all federally protected classes.[19] Some cities have them, and all states do. Bring all your documentation. You also might consult a lawyer to see if you have a case for discrimination.

---

19 "Who is protected from employment discrimination?" US Equal Employment Opportunity Commission www.eeoc.gov/employers/small-business/3-who-protected-employment-discrimination.

- *Deal with the severance offer, if you get one* (not every woman is working in a job with this "benefit"). Everyone over forty is legally entitled to twenty-one days to review a severance agreement, so most companies just extend that time period to all employees. Review the offer as soon as possible with family, loved ones, friends, or legal counsel. An online resource is Sklover Working Wisdom,[20] a site with information for employees to "level the playing field" with employers.

- *If you don't get a severance offer, you can still ask for severance pay.* If there is a severance policy at your company, you can ask for compliance with that policy. If there isn't, see if you can ask former colleagues and find out what, if anything, they or others in your company received. They may not be able to tell you, as many separation agreements say you cannot discuss the terms with anyone other than a lawyer, accountant, a spouse, or one family member. At very least, see if you can find out your industry standard. For many companies, a rule of thumb is two weeks' severance for every year worked.

- *Negotiate what you and your employer will say about your departure.*

---

20   Skloverworkingwisdom.com.

AFTER THE SHOCK HAS WORN OFF

We can't tell you when this will be. One day, you will feel less stunned, but may still need to manage the hurt.

- Read *Transitions* by William Bridges to gain some compassionate perspective on what's happening to you.

- Read *Daring Greatly* by Brené Brown to understand how this experience can help make you strong.

- Find a skilled listener who can help you manage and sort out your emotions: a therapist, LCSW, NP, psychiatrist, clergy, etc.—someone you connect with.

- Work with a compassionate, experienced career coach to recover your confidence.

- Find or form a group of people (women) who have experienced job loss and are recovering from it.

- When you are ready, get and use *What Color Is Your Parachute?*, *Designing Your Life*, *Your Right Fit Job*, or one of the multitudes of self-help job search/ career exploration books in the marketplace.

  - "Ready" is when this experience doesn't feel "hot" any longer. You no longer want to weep or gnash your teeth. You have settled enough to accept that it is time to face what's next.

- As much as possible, present a positive, professional attitude to the work world. This will help you feel positive. It turns out that work is also about how you deal with what gets thrown your way.

Reflecting on our own experiences and the stories of our contributors, there are a few more practical suggestions for you to consider in the intermediate period after being let go that we hope will help you reclaim your personal power.

- *Give yourself structure*. Create a schedule for your day, a plan or your "to dos," which can be things like going to a gym or meeting a friend. Get out of the house, make plans with people, seek company instead of isolation.

- *Speak carefully and wisely*. Resist the temptation to speak badly in public forums about your previous employer or boss because, as you know, professional worlds tend to be small and any negativity will be to your detriment. If it happens, forgive yourself. These are difficult times, and you are suffering.

- *Seek out books that describe how emotional stress works on the brain* and how emotions operate in the workplace, such as *Emotional Intelligence*, *Primal Leadership*, *The Emotional Brain*, or *Leading Brains*.[21] These can give you insight and tools to empower you in your job search and next job.

---

21 See Additional Helpful Resources.

- *We are saying this again to make the point: Treat yourself with the kindness you would give someone who has suffered a huge loss or traumatic event* (because you have). Eat healthy food. Sleep. Drink water. Get physically active—take a walk, ride a bicycle, hike, swim—whatever soothes you. Watch funny movies or shows or videos; laughing can help you come back to life.

- *If possible, take some time before launching into a job search.* You need some time to transition emotionally from your previous job and to recover a bit from the trauma of being betrayed by work. The time you need is individual—some women need a week, some need a month, while others need more time. The key is to begin a search when you are ready to present yourself with confidence in your talents, skills, and ability to contribute. The right career coach can help you regain your confidence.

- *If you suffer from feeling shame after losing your job, the collective experience from these stories suggests that you reach out and connect with someone you love, who loves you right back.* Tell them your story. And then tell another person, and another. Or, if it feels right, get together with friends, like many of our contributors did. Go where it's warm. You know in your gut who is safe for you. Talking may help you identify the messages or expectations driving your shame. Professionals who work with shame can provide further insight into how you can move through it.

HANDLING A JOB INTERRUPTION ON YOUR RESUME

There is a distinction to be made between having a job and having work. The good news is that with more and more people "gigging" and contracting and the job losses due to COVID, it seems like having a JOB (being employed full-time) is less common than it was.[22]

When you are able, make a business card, form an LLC, and identify yourself as a consultant. There are people who need you and your skills and there is work to be done! If you don't want to form an LLC, you can still call yourself a consultant. For example, if you help a friend with a business question or project *pro bono* (for free), you may call yourself a consultant—this is work. We know women who work entirely in this way: finding enough money and healthcare benefits is stressful, but they love the work they do and the schedule it allows.

There are many legitimate reasons for a break in having a full-time JOB. Several contributors had family members who needed care. Some decided to go back to school and change their focus. Some of our contributors took a hiatus because they could. Employers accept these reasons. The point here is not to deny that this situation needs to be finessed, but

---

22   As an aside, we love Dan Price's Tweet from 13 October 2020: *no minimum wage *no health benefits *no retirement plan *no unemployment benefits *no sick days *no vacation time *no paid leave—the "gig economy" just sounds like companies found a way to rebrand "working in the year 1890."

rather to say that having an authentic story is enough to keep you moving forward.

THINKING AHEAD

We encourage you to think ahead when you take a job, and while you are working in any job. Being aware that any job can end at any time is a suit of armor that helps us be strong and prepared for whatever might happen at work. This collection of stories conveys that our work lives need careful awareness: even though you may emulate the best version of your position, everything can be taken from you in an instant for reasons that you may not understand, and/or are beyond your control. We can all be betrayed by work at any time.

Here is the start of your work survival kit.

- Have a personal phone, even if you also have a business phone from your employer, so you will always be able to communicate.

- Have a "go bag" or a "go file" of things—or at least a list of things—that you will take home if you have to leave immediately.

- Send yourself copies of documents (no company secrets, please) that highlight your work strengths, so you have samples of your work.

- Send email addresses of meaningful business contacts to your personal email so you can reach out to your network on your own terms.

- Have a personal email as your LinkedIn email, not a business email, so you always have access to it.

- Find an employment lawyer and keep the name in your contacts.

- If possible, have savings or credit cards that can cover at least three months of expenses.

- Have a tribe of trusted friends outside of your work circle.

- Keep your resume up to date with work or projects that matter to you.

- Keep active with and build your network. When you meet someone new, add them to your LinkedIn connections, and send a quick personal note.

- Every organization has a handbook of benefits. Read yours. Know what you are entitled to because you work there. This will include the company's severance policy, if it has one, and COBRA specifics.

- Define yourself, own your skills, and separate your identity from your job. Doing this often creates an empowered sense of hope and agency.

Chapter 27

FOLKS DON'T KNOW WHAT TO SAY

While this book is aimed primarily at women who have been fired, there may be readers who have friends and relatives who have been fired and want to be supportive. When the women in this book were fired, people wanted to be kind when responding to this information. Yet it can be awkward. Few know what to say or do when a woman says she's been fired.

We have suggestions (below), but it's important to be aware that there are things women hate hearing. Even though the intent behind offering these adages is to offer comfort, the actual sentiment rings hollow: it doesn't make us feel better and can diminish our experience. These statements may serve to distance the listener from the impact of the event and help them cope, but that does not help the person who just got let go!

For women who have been fired, in the spirit of validation and raising awareness, we've listed some of the most common things that people say and responses you can think to yourself to help you keep your sense of composure. We don't recommend saying any of these aloud, unless you want to alienate people with good hearts who mean well, so just say, "Thank you" or some variation and move on.

- "Don't take it personally, it's only business." *Of course it's personal! What could be more personal than my job?! This affects my selfhood and my livelihood.*

- "I know how you feel." *No, you don't. (Unless you have also been fired.)*

- "You'll find something else, don't worry." *Can you help me find something else right now so I can pay my bills, help my mom, afford my family health insurance, save for my kids' college or my retirement so I don't worry?*

- "In five years, you'll look back and realize that this was for the best." *How do you know?!!? That doesn't help me now!! I wish it were five years from now!*

- "Getting fired may be one of the best things that ever happened to you." *Yeah, maybe, but not today! You saying this when I am so upset devalues the experience and where I am in this process right now.*

- "What doesn't kill you makes you stronger." *How do you know this isn't killing me? And who thought that I needed to be stronger anyway?* You can say, "Then I guess I'll be Superwoman soon."

- "Don't feel sorry for yourself." *I get to feel as sorry for myself as I want! Please have respect for my healing process.*

- "You're so resilient." *What choice do I have?*

- "Celebrate!" *It's hard to celebrate losing my income when I have a family and bills, and there aren't a lot of jobs on my horizon.* You can say, "Maybe next year."

- "Send me your resume tomorrow." *This is actually very helpful, so thank you, yet I don't have a resume and haven't looked for a job in a long time, and I'm hurting. Can you give me more time?* You can say, "Thank you. Can I get it to you next week, so I have a chance to polish it up?"

- "It's going to be hard to find something in your field (or at your age)." *Really? Tell me something I don't know and stop scaring me—I do a good enough job of that myself.*

- "The best revenge is getting a great job." *How am I going to do that? And I'm a little nervous about whether I can get a great job now that I've been fired. Plus, I don't want revenge. I liked my job and now I do want another one but not to "show" anyone anything—except maybe myself that I still have skill and ability that are valued by others.* You can say, "Thank you. I hope I can count on your support when I start networking."

HELPFUL THINGS TO SAY TO SOMEONE WHO'S LOST HER JOB

- I am so sorry. That stinks. That sounds unfair. How can I help?

- Being fired is horrible. It is one of the worst things that can happen.

- I would love to listen if you would like to tell me your story...when you are ready. Coffee's on me.

- Think of yourself as a person with gifts that need to be shared in a different environment than you were in.

- It's their loss, because you are terrific; they are not worthy of you.

- There's nothing wrong with you.

- *Your variation of a hug and* I love you.

- I know this great book, entitled *Betrayed by Work*... It can help you see that you are not alone.

- The feelings that you have right now will end; this will come to an end.

- It may take you some time to come to your own peace with what happened. That is okay and part of healing.

- Let me know how I can help—I am here for you.

Chapter 28

WHAT WE HAVE LEARNED: THE PERSONAL

This is a book about being betrayed by work. It's about how professional women were fired, how they felt when they lost their jobs, and the damage done to them as a result of how they were treated. There is an interval between getting fired and being emotionally ready to apply for new work.

It is an emotional span, a period of experiencing strong and difficult feelings that need to be managed—because they don't rapidly subside—before we can move forward with them under control. This emotional span is unaccounted for by experts and even by our contributors themselves. If we do not tend to this emotional interval before embarking on what comes next, we may not heal. For those who do not address it, the unacknowledged pain can carry over indefinitely.

This experience, this deep jolt, does not resolve in the same way for everyone, and many only move forward after experiencing deep darkness. For some women who get fired and move on, sooner rather than later, life turns out to be better than before. For others, it becomes a hard path fraught with sorrow, difficulty, or lingering negative feelings that haunt and perhaps limit subsequent work options. We hope these stories underscore how dramatic this experience can be.

The trauma of being betrayed by work translates for many women into disempowerment, shame, and fear of retribution. Among the women we asked to share their stories of being fired, quite a few would not do so. Some were still too upset about being let go. Some were still too busy trying to find a new job. Some were afraid that talking to us would put their current position in jeopardy. And some were too freshly on a new path to be able to reflect with any perspective.

To emphasize this point, when we were trying to find an agent and publisher for this book, one of the agents responded with the common pejorative question: *What did these women do to get themselves fired?*

This response was heartbreaking and infuriating. As you now know, none of the women here did anything to merit the treatment they received. Perhaps it was time for them to leave their jobs. Perhaps they were no longer good fits (for example, Melanie even realized she was not a good fit with the corporate world). But to have to field questions like the above (what did *you* do?), after the indignity and cruelty to which all were subjected? Well, it still leaves both of us dumbfounded.

A personality conflict, a change of leadership, gender bias, unacknowledged racism, a "too high" salary, toxic work culture, power plays—these were the reasons our contributors were fired. Yes, in some cases, there may have been a small mistake or minor error in judgment.

But these things happen and are typically overlooked or gently addressed and then forgotten—by a friendly boss, at a company with stable leadership and sound financial condition, in a collegial environment with a learning mindset where back-stabbing and undermining are not the norm, or at a conscious workplace where all employees—not just white men—are afforded the same rights to professional support and promotion.

We need to pay attention to what happens when women are fired. Here are key themes and thoughts that emerged from our collection of stories.

PERSONAL PAIN

For professional women who identified strongly with their jobs, the hurt of not seeing it coming was devastating. The personal pain was compounded by the manner in which they were let go. It cut across job types, personality characteristics, stages in life, race, and ethnic background. The magnitude of hurt surprised them, so much so that we began to wonder: What is it about being betrayed by work that is so painful and takes so long to recover from?

The knowledge that it is a top-ten stressful life event (number eight on the Holmes & Rahe Stress Scale[23]) doesn't fully capture the essence of the experience. What else is at play?

---

23   See the Pain Doctor, "Top 10 Most Stressful Life Events: The Holmes and Rahe Stress Scale," March 2, 2018 paindoctor.com/top-10-stressful-life-events-holmes-rahe-stress-scale.

BETRAYAL

Betrayal is at the root of much of the pain of being fired. As we said in Chapter 1, "betray" means *to deliver or expose to an enemy by treachery or disloyalty; to disappoint the hopes or expectations of; be disloyal to*. "Betrayal" means a violation of a person's trust or confidence, violation of a moral standard. A betrayal is enacted upon someone who has no control over what is happening to them.

There is no shortage of nonfiction or fictional betrayals in the Western literary canon. Caesar and Brutus, Jesus and Judas, Gollum and Frodo, Benedict Arnold and the fledgling United States—across genres and epochs, betrayal is widely recognized as a terrible thing.

We found academic literature about personal betrayal by family members, significant others, or acquaintances; betrayals that are deeply intimate, surprising, poignant, destructive, and crushing. But they are in a different realm than being betrayed by work, about which we found almost no conceptual material written.

This gap surprised us because the workplace is the primary environment in which most adults operate daily. This is where many of us derive meaning. What happens at work affects our ability to function as adults.

Self-determination theory[24] posits that people at work are motivated by competence, autonomy, *and* relatedness.

---

24   Marylene Gagne & Edward L. Deci, " Self Determination Theory and Work Motivation, Journal of Organizational Behavior, 26, 331-362 (2005) selfdeterminationtheory.org/SDT/documents/2005_GagneDeci_JOB_SDTtheory.pdf.

In *Your Brain at Work*,[25] David Rock proposes a five-factor model of social interaction derived from social cognitive neuroscience called *SCARF*: Status, Certainty, Autonomy, Relatedness, and Fairness. In the workplace, people want to feel important, safe, in control, and included and be treated fairly in relation to everyone else. When leaders have these elements in place, they build trust with their employees.

Getting fired shatters every single one of the SCARF elements.

Being betrayed by work violates real human needs. Suddenly, women were no longer important (S), their positions were no longer safe (C), they had no control over their fate (A), they were excluded from the workplace and the people in it (R), and there was no opportunity to meaningfully dispute the decision of the firing (F).

Getting fired was a final decision, and out they went.

Not only were these women cast out, but in many instances, other members of their work tribe plotted behind their backs to get rid of them. At very least, their boss and HR were deciding things in secret. This behind-the-scenes strategizing created lingering, long-term distrust among all parties in the workplace, including those left behind.

This ruptured trust is not easily repaired. Women who get fired have a difficult time again trusting a) themselves, b) other employers, or c) clients, if they go on to be consultants. At the workplace, employees left behind are less apt to trust that they will be treated any better in the

---

25   David Rock, Your Brain at Work, New York: Harper Business, 2009.

future. This observation is validated through the SCARF model lens: when all or most of the SCARF elements are missing or discarded, trust is destroyed.

Work is a "defining framework within which we set priorities and make decisions about other important facets of our lives"[26] These stories reveal how suddenly losing this defining framework can catalyze stress reactions and trauma, because it is a violation of the social contract we expect from the workplace.[27] Several of our contributors displayed symptoms consistent with trauma. Rage. Shame. Feelings of powerlessness.

So. Much. Personal. Pain.

We need to pay attention.

SHAME

A common refrain from many of our contributors after getting let go was *I felt so ashamed*. Shame is an emotion of self-blame: it is "the uncomfortable sensation we feel in the pit of our stomach when it seems we have no safe haven from the judging gaze of others. We feel small and bad about

---

26   Herminia Ibarra, Working Identity: Unconventional Strategies for Reinventing Your Career, Boston: Harvard Business Review Press, 2004.

27   Including betrayal trauma, abandonment trauma and adjustment disorder. Freyd's Betrayal Trauma Theory framework, although not yet explicitly applied to being fired, also stands as a model through which the trauma of getting fired can be understood, particularly the sensitivity to a violation of social contracts. See Freyd, Jennifer J. (2020), What is Betrayal Trauma? What is Betrayal Trauma Theory? dynamic.uoregon.edu/jjf/defineBT.html.

ourselves and wish we could vanish."[28] We are: Small. Bad. Inferior. Isolated. Powerless.[29]

We did not find any literature precisely about shame and unexpected job loss, but we did find the description by Brené Brown, PhD, of women's experience of shame:[30] "Shame often produces overwhelming and painful feelings of confusion, fear, anger, judgment, and/or the need to hide." Brown found that women experienced shame by feeling trapped, powerless, and psychologically isolated, feelings expressed by women in this book.[31]

Brown's observation that "most people subscribe to the belief that shame is a good tool for keeping people in line"[32] shines a new light on the entire HR model of terminations in the United States as a system of control. The ways in which women were let go compounded the shame they felt from losing their job in the first place. Humiliating them on their way out the door was a way to pile on the shame.

The damage that shame does to women is not commensurate with the intention of "keeping people in line." In our small set of contributors, there are women

---

28   Kaemmerer, A. Behavior and Society: The Scientific Underpinnings and Impacts of Shame, Scientific American, August 9, 2019, www.scientificamerican.com/article/the-scientific-underpinnings-and-impacts-of-shame.

29   Tangney, J.P. & Dearing, R. L. Shame and Guilt. New York: The Guilford Press (2002).

30   Brown, Brene. Shame Resilience Theory: A Grounded Theory Study on Women and Shame. Families in Society: The Journal of Contemporary Social Services, 87 (1), 43–52 (2006).

31   Brown describes a web of shame that is full of shoulds. These are not necessarily our own shoulds, but instead are rigid expectations from our socio-cultural environment, such as what we should be, how we should be, or who we should be. Her idea is that shame occurs when some of those 'shoulds' get violated.

32   Brown, Brene. Daring Greatly. New York: Gotham Books (2012), p. 72–73.

who have not fully healed, women who remain so afraid of being punished by a former employer or field in which they work that they did not use their real names in this book, and women who changed fields altogether because they simply felt too much shame to remain in their previous one.

Remember, too, there were women who were still too afraid to speak to us, even after being assured of anonymity. Multiply our small set by the thousands of women who get fired every year, and we can begin to infer the scale of devastation wrought among the psyches of women shamed and humiliated by the way they are treated by employers dispensing with their services.

Brown tells us that shame is associated with many negative outcomes and no positive ones, and is certainly not effective as a "helpful compass for good behavior."[33] Do employers really intend to cause such deep and long-lasting damage when they fire people? We hope not. That would be a shameful thing to do!

It's well past time to change the way people lose their jobs. The shame-inducing practices employed need to be exposed and eliminated, or at minimum, altered.

Brown's Shame Resilience Theory states that at the other end of the shame continuum is empathy, connection, power, and freedom.[34] This sounds like what many of our women contributors told us they experienced when they shared their stories with us and with others. Their feelings of shame

33   Brown, Brene. Daring Greatly. New York: Gotham Books (2012), p. 72–73.
34   Brown, Brene. Shame Resilience Theory: A Grounded Theory Study on Women and Shame. Families in Society: The Journal of Contemporary Social Services, 87(1), 43–52 (2006).

began to diminish. They showed us that shame cannot live once it is brought into the light.

Shame is just one of many emotions that show up in the stories we collected. In fact, "emotions" are an important theme throughout all our stories: experiencing them, accepting them, learning how to work through them, and ultimately being able to use them to propel us forward.

PERSONAL TRANSFORMATION

Clarissa Pinkola Estes, PhD, tells us about jack pine trees in her *Dangerous Old Woman* series. Jack pine seeds are released only under conditions of extreme heat, such as fire. Without fire, the seeds are not released. Without fire, new trees will not grow.

The contributors of these stories encountered fire in their lives, and for many, this caused an opening to personal transformation. Some opened to new experiences, while others were cracked open so wide, they moved forward to new work and a new sense of self.

The latter group's metamorphosis was built on a great deal of pain, loss, reflection, and acceptance of change. But what exactly took place? Many reported feelings of betrayal and hopelessness. Others reported having lost their moorings, and even their identity. This meant living and working in a state of confusion and unresolved emotions—taking jobs that didn't fit, searching for work seemingly forever, missing a sense of purpose, and feeling depressed and disoriented.

The women here experienced some or all of these difficulties for varying amounts of time and with different degrees of intensity. As they came out of this dark time, all had a deepened self-knowledge, a new sense of strength, and more compassion and empathy for themselves and others. They realized that they could survive. And indeed, they have survived.

Compassion and empathy may be the most important transformative traits that emerged from these experiences. The experience of being deeply hurt and having to feel their way through to another place gave these women a visceral understanding of what it is like to be treated badly, and in fact, as less than human. In sharing their stories and the emotional journey they took, our contributors learned the power of their stories to help themselves and others emerge more whole and stronger. Emotions became the currency of healing, rather than something to be avoided, denied, or shut down. The motivation for telling their stories became twofold: to help other women who have similar experiences, and to change the dysfunctional system that produces such human devastation.

And yet.

Many of our contributors report lingering distrust, resentment (re-feeling), and wariness of others. A few reported a deep scar robbing them of some fundamental strength or lessened joy in life. Some have lingering self-doubt about their abilities. Most are now careful to look out for themselves because it's clear to them that no one else, starting with their employer, has their best interests in mind. And some remain unable to trust anything or anybody at work, and even other parts of their lives. These are some of the unhappy truths about the aftermath of women being abruptly dismissed from their jobs.

Would personal transformation still have occurred if firings were handled more compassionately? We can't know. We wonder what else our contributors might have accomplished professionally if so much of their emotional energy had not been used up by healing the deep wounds of a noncompassionate firing.

Being fired likely can't be 100 percent pain-free.[35] But it probably can be constructed such that, instead of destroying some fundamental part of ourselves and holding us back, it leaves us in a state where we can use the pain as a transformative experience to lead us forward to new possibilities. Although this is a book about women, we believe this concept holds for men, too.

In reviewing the stories herein, it seems clear that the specific goal of at least some of the firings was to shame and punish the women involved: to destroy their power and influence in their workplaces (and, by indirect extension, their fields), as well as aspects of themselves. The people who fired our contributors did them harm. But our contributors chose to transform their pain into a launching pad toward a new phase of their work lives.

We hope such transformative experiences will not be limited to the few who are fundamentally resilient but will become the norm.

---

35   Scott, Kim, Radical Candor. New York: St. Martin's Press, 2017. P. 66–70, 189–193. Scott also realizes the pain inherent in this process and we feel hopeful by her observation that letting someone go creates new possibilities for them.

Chapter 29

WHAT WE HAVE LEARNED: THE WORKPLACE

Firing happens in a context: the workplace, and in particular the American workplace. Our stories reveal themes about emotions, power, leadership, and the culture of work that shape how the termination process is handled and that need alteration.

EMOTIONS

The American workplace is not set up to accommodate emotions: particularly not those perceived by our society as negative emotions, definitely not women's negative emotions, and especially not emotions that make us feel vulnerable. This conclusion was inescapable and tragic, because being fired, laid off, or downsized causes strong emotions among those let go and those who remain.

Tony Schwartz observed that "Most employers don't give emotions much attention either, preferring that we park them at the door in the morning so they don't get in the way during the workday." One of his readers, M., shared this telling comment: "Do many people have the luxury of either job security or a professional and collegial work environment to be able to do this? I don't see how 'naming your emotions' in the workplace can do anything other than allow that information to be used against you. **Particularly if you are female.**"[36]

M's comment amplifies that it is, indeed, perilous for women to express our emotions at work. Research extends this observation to "negative" emotions.

Salerno and Peter-Hagene (2015)[37] articulate what many of us sensed: women lose influence and credibility when getting angry, while men gain both. This finding underscores Brescoll and Uhlmann's (2008) work which showed that lower status and lower wages were conferred upon women who showed anger at work, while anger demonstration heightened the status of men.[38]

In other words, in the workplace, men can express a wider range of emotions than women and are even rewarded for expressing so-called negative emotions like anger and frustration. Women are punished for expressing the same emotions. We are held to a different standard of behavior, even by other women who have absorbed these dominant societal attitudes.

---

36   "The Importance of Naming Your Emotions," Life@Work column, *New York Times*, April 3, 2015, www.nytimes.com/2015/04/04/business/dealbook/the-importance-of-naming-your-emotions.html.

37   Salerno, JM, Peter-Hagene LC. One angry woman: Anger expression increases influence for men, but decreases influence for women, during group deliberation. Law and Human Behavior, 39 (6), (2015) 581–592.

38   VL Brescoll, EL Uhlmann. "Can an angry woman get ahead? Status conferral, gender, and expression of emotion in the workplace," *Psychological Science*, Vol 19, Issue 3 (2008), pp 268–275. journals.sagepub.com/doi/abs/10.1111/j.1467-9280.2008.02079.x.

When the women here were fired, their most immediate reactions were anger and fear, but they weren't "allowed" to express either. There was no acceptable way for them to convey the fear that emerged, nor that it was paralyzing and difficult to suppress. Nor that the anger or rage was so intense as to override their ability to think clearly and function wisely. The overpowering message from the workplace is that women should not have these feelings, much less express them. We may stuff them down or suck them up and not make a fuss. We are supposed to leave quietly and nicely. Once we are off the premises, we may have our feelings.

The most grotesque distortion is that some of us feel bad about ourselves because we expressed our emotions in some way in the moment of being fired that conveyed that we weren't "good girls."

FIRING AFFECTS EVERYONE

In the current model of firing, both sides—the person delivering and the person receiving the news—experience anger and fear; the net effect is toxic. We've already discussed what happens to the person receiving the news. Now let's quickly look across the table.

Firing someone is scary; most people have never done it. The person delivering the news in a typical emotion-averse workplace has likely been advised by HR professionals and lawyers to avoid expressing any sympathy or empathy, lest a lawsuit for unlawful termination be built on those words. They have a limited script where they are not empowered to answer specific questions. They may treat the woman getting fired like an enemy who needs to be expelled. They are afraid.[39] And, after the deed is done, the person can commiserate with someone about how hard it was to let someone go, which dissipates their discomfort and fear.

Brown's "armoring up" means convincing yourself that the other person is somehow guilty or worthy of mistreatment.[40] It's a strategy that can be employed in preparation for perceived conflict. We wonder if the people who fire women as in the above scenario "armor up" first, an approach that would certainly help them avoid uncomfortable feelings.

The colleagues of the fired woman who remain behind are expected to hide their emotions. Often an email goes out from HR stating that the woman who was fired is no longer with the company, no reason given. This email only serves to generate whispers in the hallways, because people want to know what happened and will speculate. It's completely natural to want to talk through the initial shock of a colleague being fired, but no one can do it openly in an emotion-averse workplace. Instead, the event is shrouded in secrecy, and as a result, people get the message that getting fired is bad and shameful. Those left behind know what to expect if they get fired.

The current method of firing people in the United States leaves emotional scars on those who were dismissed and on those who remain. This approach eats away at people's

---

39   Scott, Kim, Radical Candor. New York: St. Martin's Press (2017). p. 66. She describes a "successful" person who claims he wakes up in a cold sweat when he has to fire someone.

40   Brene Brown, Daring Greatly, NY: Avery, 2012. p 201.

attachment and loyalty to, and trust in, their employer. The workplace must evolve beyond avoiding or denying the existence of the emotions triggered by sudden job loss.

POWER

The stories in this book call attention to what it is like to be on the receiving end of power brandished in the workplace. They reveal power wielded irresponsibly: without full awareness of, or care about, the resultant damage or destructive effects enacted upon the recipients.

The stories also reveal the limits of individual power. None of the women here had enough power to save their jobs or to determine the manner in which they were let go. They had illusory power during the time they worked—based on being told by deed or in words that they were valued, needed, or important to the work. Some even managed other people and had a say over others' fates in the workplace. But, when it came to having power over their own fate, those illusions came down with a crash.

Women experienced immediate powerlessness: their control over what was happening to them was instantaneously ripped away. This experience alone was terrifying. It destroyed their perception of themselves as valued individuals or persons with agency and undermined their belief in their ability to shape their lives. Powerlessness reduced their ability to withstand the blow of being fired.

In an instant, someone else changed their lives and fates— and not in a direction they would have chosen.

One dark side of power in the workplace is the traumatization, victimization, and destruction of women that occurs when they are on the receiving end of bosses wielding power corruptly and with cruelty. Corruption is believing one's actions are justified because they are the wise and necessary thing to do, while rejecting views other than one's own. Cruelty is "callous indifference to causing pain and suffering"[41] which is legitimized by such thoughts as "this is what the lawyers say we have to do."

The entire firing system is stacked against the woman who gets fired, with many ways of rendering her powerless. For example, severance agreements typically include clauses stipulating that she may talk to *one* person (not two!) about the proposed separation agreement being put before her. One person. As we have witnessed, losing one's job reverberates deeply within and beyond ourselves. It may affect an entire family. Perhaps you are single and don't have family. Who do you speak with? Can a newly fired person have any perspective on the situation without being able to discuss the options being placed before them with their people?

This seems like bullying. What could an employer be so afraid of that they insist on this strange limit?

Legal agreements are constructed to ward off any possible threat to the employer from the woman who has been fired. Employers include "non-disparagement" clauses in agreements that require the former employee to refrain from bad-mouthing the employer in any way in the future. Employers often refuse mutual non-disparagement clauses, even when the woman has been fired for no stated reason. It gets worse: to get any

---

41   Definition www.google.com/
search?q=cruelty&oq=cruelty&aqs=chrome..69i57j0l5.1919j0j4&sourceid=chrome&ie=UTF-8.

severance payment, the woman (former employee) usually has to agree to surrender her right to sue for wrongful termination or other legal action against the company. The employer is unwilling to surrender any power or control.

It's curious how much fear lies behind the current system of firing people. Employers construct armored walls of legalese to protect themselves from the employee they have just stripped of everything: her livelihood, colleagues, reputation, and identity. What really can a woman who got fired do to a company?

WHITE SUPREMACY AND STRUCTURAL RACISM

Structural racism is a system designed to maintain the power of white people at the expense of Black people, indigenous people, and other people of color (BIPOC). The gist of white supremacy culture[42] is that there are defining characteristics of a system that are meant to keep people of color powerless, such as Perfectionism, Sense of Urgency, Defensiveness, Quantity over Quality, Worship of the Written Word, Only One Right Way, Paternalism, Fear of Open Conflict, Individualism, Progress is Bigger, More, or Right to Comfort.

Characteristics of white supremacy culture are close to those of the "command and control" or "'winner take all"

---

42   See White Supremacy Culture Characteristics www.showingupforracialjustice.org/white-supremacy-culture-characteristics.html and Dismantling Racism: A Workbook for Social Change Groups, by Kenneth Jones and Tema Okun, ChangeWork, 2001.

culture that characterizes much of the American workplace, or, as we think of it, bad leadership and bad management within an emotion-averse culture. These methods of systematic control are the mechanisms through which straight, cisgender white men and their allies maintain power and privilege. It makes sense that the workplace is the locus of these mechanisms, because money is a main and visible source of power and control.

Many writers and researchers document that companies with more diversity outperform those with less, and yet there has been little change in the control and management of public companies. As history has shown, there is little incentive for those with power to give it up. Corporate boards remain controlled by white men: among the three thousand largest publicly traded corporations, 87 percent of board members are white, and 80 percent are men.[43] As a direct consequence, most CEOs are also white men.

A Wall Street Journal article[44] reported that slightly less than 1 percent, or a total of four chief executives running America's top five hundred companies are Black. Black executives hold only 3 percent (one in thirty-three) of the C-suite positions that are often seen as a prerequisite to the top job. Just one in five C-suite positions are held by women, and one in twenty-five C-suite positions are held by women of color.[45] Even fewer gay and lesbian, and far

43   Peter Eavis, "Diversity Push Barely Budges Corporate Boards to 12.5 percent, Survey Finds." The New York Times, 9/15/2020 www.nytimes.com/2020/09/15/business/economy/corporate-boards-black-hispanic-directors.html.

44   Te-Ping Chen, "Why Are There Still So Few Black CEOs," The Wall Street Journal, 9/28/2020 www.wsj.com/articles/why-are-there-still-so-few-black-ceos-11601302601.

45   Jess Huang, Alexis Krivkovich, Irina Starikova, Lareina Yee and Delia Zanoschi, Women in the Workplace 2019, McKinsey & Company, October 2019 www.mckinsey.

fewer transgender people are in the C-suite or serving on corporate boards. This is a pipeline problem, or a "broken rung" problem, where fewer non-white and non-male individuals get promoted to managerial positions. From there, it's a slow reduction in those who advance to the next step on the leadership ladder.

The 2019 McKinsey report on Women in the Workplace notes that:

> women of color, lesbian and bisexual women, and women with disabilities are having distinct—and by and large worse—experiences than women overall. Most notably, Black women and women with disabilities face more barriers to advancement, get less support from managers, and receive less sponsorship than other groups of women.

The dearth of Black people, people of color, and women in all shapes and sizes in positions of power in the workplace reveals that structural racism and sexism are alive and well. The Black women in our book clearly experienced its effects and felt they were fired for both being a woman and a Black person. Other women of color felt similar vulnerability. We heard over and over from our women colleagues and friends, *I know so many women who have been discriminated against due to:*

Race. Weight. Gender. Ethnicity. Looks. Disability. Age.

---

com/featured-insights/gender-equality/women-in-the-workplace-2019, page 8.

It's saddening and infuriating. The workplace is set up by design to ensure that power does not become a shared resource. Only certain people can gain power.

LEADERSHIP

Leaders set the tone for organizations. Leadership is a critical factor in determining how women are separated from their jobs. We didn't see emotionally intelligent or compassionate leaders in these stories. Perhaps this is due to a general misperception about what leadership really is, and that the people who are most prone to misinterpret leadership are also those who seek out leadership positions. Perhaps it is due to our current culture of work, which rewards getting things done at the expense of people and relationships and too often puts profit and power before people. Perhaps it is a combination of all of these things. Whatever the cause, we found bad leadership abundantly on display by bosses in these stories.

We came to understand that being a boss does not make you a *good leader*.

Bad bosses exerted their power in self-serving ways. They fired women to retain or grow their power, to advance themselves, and/or to diminish their staff. Some bosses were a toxic extension of a toxic organizational culture. Some were racist. Some thought it was their way or no way. Some were cruel.

Bosses defined gaining and keeping their position and visibility as more important than how they worked with others. These bosses may have been hugely successful and delivered "wins" to the company, but that success was likely at great expense to others.

The converse—good leadership—was articulated by some women as what they were missing in their bosses. Most people at work are motivated more by recognition and appreciation of their contribution and efforts and less by money.[46] Perhaps there just hasn't been enough modeling how to acknowledge and appreciate subordinates' work for bosses to understand what it means, how to do it, and how important it is. Our contributors tell us that good leaders focus on both the work and the well-being of individuals. They amplify the positive aspects of themselves and others. They are confident in their own abilities, they are comfortable with the power they possess, and they are compassionate with other people and their lives and circumstances. They are aware of the power inherent in their role and wield it responsibly and compassionately instead of destructively.[47]

Good leadership doesn't co-opt people's personal power; rather, good leaders encourage people to tap into and develop their own personal power. They know it is important to inclusively acknowledge other people's contributions so that all can share in the pride and positive experience of a job well done. In short, good leaders showcase the accomplishments of those individuals they lead, take credit

---

46   Katzenback JR, Khan Z. (2010). Leading Outside the Lines: How to Mobilize the Informal Organization, Energize Your Team, and Get Better Results. www.forbes.com/2010/04/06/money-motivation-pay-leadership-managing-employees.html.
47   We focus on good leadership because the word leadership is insufficient. After all, there are leaders who one would not call good, e.g. Hitler, Chile's General Pinochet, and Cambodia's Pol Pot, to name a few who led followers to horrific goals.

in the form of the entire team taking credit, and credit the entire team. They understand and respect the responsibility of furthering employees' careers in ways that benefit the employees. Good leaders are often invisible in the process and will say "Thank you" at the end.[48]

What might good leadership look like in practice? We're inspired by Robert Reid's cultural philosophy. He is chief executive at Intacct, and notes that:

> Almost everyone goes to work to do a good job. And if they're not doing a good job, most organizations step back and say, "I'm not sure they're going to make it here." We think the opposite—that we've done something to let them down. We either haven't taken them through the right process or trained them appropriately. If somebody is not doing something the way you expect or you have a different viewpoint, you need to seek to understand what's going on and help them. [49]

We love this thinking and can only infer how this philosophy would have changed the lives of the women we interviewed for this collection of stories.

Imagine if companies assumed responsibility for having to fire someone because they did not provide appropriate

---

48   After all these years, we still love "Leadership is an Art" by Max DePree (New York: Currency, 2004). Leaders say 'thank you' at the end. www.amazon.com/Leadership-Art-Max-Depree/dp/0385512465.

49   Two current concepts of leadership are "resonant leadership" and "emotional intelligence." Resonant leadership is explored in Boyatsis R, McKee A (2005). Resonant Leadership, Boston, MA: Harvard Business School Press. Emotional intelligence is discussed by Daniel Goleman in various books, including Goleman D, Boyatsis R & McKee A (2013). Primal Leadership: Unleashing the Power of Emotional Intelligence, Boston, MA: Harvard Business Review Press, 2013.

leadership for the person to do their job properly. Imagine if companies had to think like Scott did and say upon parting, "We did not match our needs to your magnificent abilities and skills," instead of supporting the "Hire slowly, fire quickly" approach found among entrepreneurs such as Bruce Poon Tip, founder of G Adventures.[50] Poon Tip and others are correct in saying organizations must make it easy for people to leave, and to support decisions to leave if the fit is not correct. However, he and others do not comprehend the human cost that accompanies the cultivation of an environment where there is simply no job security, when employees know that, any day, they could be quickly fired because the sands shift.

Imagine if we took Scott's ideas one step further and said: "We (the company) recognize that it took us X days/months/ years of your life to come to the conclusion that we did not match our needs to your magnificent abilities and skills, and this is how we will compensate you for our misjudgment." It may not be entirely realistic, but it conjures a very different scenario for the firing (and hiring) process.

Colleagues of ours have countered us by telling of difficult CEOs and noting that people had a real sense of accomplishment when working for these people. We would argue that employees had a sense of accomplishment *in spite of* the CEO's difficult personality and behavior, not *because* the way the CEO behaved was good for the people working there. Indeed, Tony Schwartz wondered "how much more these men could have enhanced thousands of people's lives—and perhaps made them even more successful—if they

---

50   documented in his book Looptail, Business Plus, 2013.

had invested as much in taking care of them as they did in conceiving great products."[51]

The work world is not a sterile environment where people can simply turn off their personhood and check all emotions at the door. In the long run, companies that expect this type of environment will pay the price in rapid turnover, unhappy, stressed-out, burned-out employees, or a generally toxic atmosphere. No one is inspired when they feel devalued.

CULTURE OF WORK

We emphasize how horribly most American workplaces treat women who are losing their jobs and how little attention gets paid to the emotional aftermath—for both the woman and the people left behind. "It's just business" is the catchphrase often used to justify this strategy. We also hear "legal reasons" for women being rapidly shuffled out without a chance to say goodbye or go back to their desk to retrieve their purse or other personal items, as if they were suddenly transformed into dangerous predators or stealth ninjas likely to do horrible damage in a subversive manner if let loose.

We've discussed factors that influence this heinous—and we believe largely unnecessary—custom, including fear of emotions, a fundamental misunderstanding of the use of power, a workplace designed to keep power in the hands of the white, male few.

---

51   Tony Schwartz, "The Bad Behavior of Visionary Leaders," The New York Times, 06/28/15 www.nytimes.com/2015/06/27/business/dealbook/the-bad-behavior-of-visionary-leaders.html.

There are a few other structural juggernauts in American work culture.

The foundational element that allows cruelly managed firing is "at will" employment, which is legal in all fifty states (with limited exceptions).[52] This is characterized as beneficial to both parties because employees are "free" to change positions whenever desired, just as employers are free to fire employees for no reason—at will. In practice, the employer benefits most from "at will" employment laws. Employment expert and former *Forbes* columnist Liz Ryan observes how much easier it is for a company to find another employee than it is for an individual to find a new job after being let go. [53]

The construction of severance agreements also emphasizes structural unfairness. Companies that do not have a severance policy will offer capriciously varied agreements based on who is being fired and the opinions of HR, the boss, and lawyers. Is it a white woman over forty? A Black man under forty? A Latinx woman over forty? Is it a gay white man over forty? Each of these people may be offered a different package based on fear of being sued, or because someone likes them better. It's murky at best.

An important aspect of culture at work involves the hiring process and its relation to firing people. Experts counsel that time spent hiring carefully will reduce the likelihood

---

52   National Conference of State Legislators, "The At-will Presumption and Exceptions to the Rule," 4/15/08 www.ncsl.org/research/labor-and-employment/at-will-employment-overview.aspx.

53   Liz Ryan, How at Will Employment Hurts Business, Forbes, May 1, 2014. www.forbes.com/sites/lizryan/2014/05/01/how-at-will-employment-hurts-business/#20ead16634d5.

of having to fire someone. Per LinkedIn, in the 2010s and 2020s, more than 80 percent of people find jobs through networking, meaning they are known to someone connected with the employer. This close connection reassures a hiring manager that a prospective employee will be a good "culture fit." In our still segregated society, this limits diversity of hiring and keeps the door closed to many talented, qualified women and people of color. Studies show that people will by nature hire people like themselves.[54]

A 2012 study found that, "the cultural similarities valued at elite professional service firms have important socioeconomic dimensions."[55] Further, because interviewers at these firms tend to be white, Ivy League-educated, upper-middle- or upper-class men and women, "the types of cultural similarities valued in elite firms' hiring processes has (*sic*) the potential to create inequalities in access to elite jobs based on parental socioeconomic status." Hiring for "culture fit" thus can be code for discriminating on the basis of gender, race, color, national origin, age, disability, etc., unless hiring managers are specifically instructed to broaden and hire a more diverse staff. And even then, unless there is a culture that actively capitalizes on diversity, people who do not fit into the dominant culture can be fired for "not fitting in." Our stories show that this happened with these Black women and women of color.

54   Rivera, Lauren. 2012. Hiring as Cultural Matching: The Case of Elite Professional Service Firms. American Sociological Review. 77: 999–1022 www.kellogg. northwestern.edu/faculty/research/researchdetail?guid=af546330-d1a7-44a7-b3ee-6f74cfe92fdb.

55   Rivera, Lauren. 2012. Hiring as Cultural Matching: The Case of Elite Professional Service Firms. American Sociological Review. 77: 999–1022. www.kellogg. northwestern.edu/faculty/research/researchdetail?guid=af546330-d1a7-44a7-b3ee-6f74cfe92fdb.

Multiple stakeholders in the world of work would benefit if there were a shift in the work culture at this critical juncture in women's employment. We advocate for consciously hiring a diverse workforce, and for radical, compassionate firing, a strategy that could create an affirmative environment by letting people know there is always a path forward that is not destructive. This would be a foundation for a flourishing, sustainable, compassionate workplace. Unless something criminal has taken place, employers could offer their employees a smooth transition to their next job, and not one that is embarrassing, humiliating, or cloaked in shame.

We got some hope that a healthier workplace is possible from the idea of mission-focused self-management.[56] The people who work in this type of structure view each other as colleagues who make agreements with one another, with peer pressure and accountability providing the structure to make this thing work. No boss can fire anyone. This self-management is based on the idea that people are fundamentally good and trustworthy.

In our tales, the assumption is the opposite, and the women who are fired are treated accordingly. We think there is a better way.

---

56   Mission-based self-management is practiced by Morning Star Tomatoes (www. morningstarco.com/). A version of it is known as holacracy (www.holacracy.org/), a management structure predicated on decision-making authority being distributed throughout the organization. It was introduced to Zappos by its late founder Tony Hsieh in 2013 where it continues to evolve (www.zapposinsights.com/about/holacracy).

Chapter 30

COMPASSIONATE FIRING: WHAT WE SUGGEST

There are situations where someone fails to do her job, or when the employee is causing more problems that he or she is solving,[57] and it makes sense for the employment relationship to end. Perhaps the job requirements have changed, and the person simply doesn't have the needed skills or the ability to learn them, even when the company has paid for sufficient training for that person to learn the skills. Perhaps the person simply does not do their job, and that situation has been discussed honestly in detail and documented over time. And of course, people who violate the law or threaten the safety of other employees do not have a place in the workplace.[58]

We do not argue with any of this. In fact, in instances other than safety or clear law-breaking, we suspect that if such a situation exists, the job is also likely also not working for the employee.

---

57   Rebecca Knight, The Right Way to Fire Someone, Harvard Business Review, 2/2/16 hbr.org/2016/02/the-right-way-to-fire-someone.
58   Be aware that in most union environments, all union members have a right to some form of notice and appeal regardless of what they have done. Make sure you know what your collective bargaining agreement says.

And yet.

Too many of the stories we heard involve women being fired for no real cause. They did not violate policies against workplace safety or discrimination. They were fired because of their personality or because their boss took a dislike to them.

- Because they challenged the status quo.

- Because there was no growth opportunity for them, and their boss felt threatened.

- Because someone else wanted to run their department or organization.

- Because they did their job too well and someone above them felt threatened.

- Because they were Black, or a woman of color, and racism stopped them from rising.

- Because being Black or a woman of color stopped them from being treated the way a white person had been treated in a similar situation, or kept managers from giving them the benefit of the doubt or compassion that white women got.

- Because arbitrary rules were applied without consideration of the actual requirements of the work being done. (Do you really need to have the person there at nine o'clock when she made sure everything was right at midnight?)

- Because, in a complicated situation, the easiest thing to do is to let the person go instead of really studying the environment and figuring out what it takes to make it right.

- Because of "optics"—how it would look to external audiences if the employer did anything else.

- Because they no longer served an employer's needs and actually needed the employer to come through for them (e.g. green card sponsorship).

- Because a top executive could claim they took action to address a systemic problem in the organization by creating a scapegoat.

These are the firings we object to and question. Not only were the reasons for firing the women in this book—and multitudes of women like them—small-minded, specious, or completely absent but, adding insult to injury, the method of firing was inhumane. It was mean and humiliating. It caused shame. And as a result, the betrayal of work relationships has gone deep for many of our contributors.

We advocate for a way to separate people from their jobs that is not destructive, shameful, or harmful. We advocate for the idea that the circumstances do not have to be completely antagonistic nor damaging to someone's overall well-being, including financial and mental. As we described in the Culture of Work section (Chapter 29), it is our impression that, as currently described, firing practices are designed to protect the employer without taking the life circumstances or feelings of the employee into account.

How might a good leader approach letting someone go?
In his blog post, "Letting People Go with Transparency and
Dignity," leadership expert Dan Rockwell[59] makes the case
for compassion and not making enemies because it may not
be necessary. Kim Scott emphasizes kindness, compassion,
and remembering that the reason you have to fire someone
is "not that they suck. It's not even that they suck at this job.
It's that this job—the job you gave them—sucks for them."[60]

Scott noted that she did not listen to her company lawyer
and treated a person with dignity when he was let go. This
resulted in the former employee not going "ballistic"—a
word chosen by the lawyer.[61] We know a woman in banking
who has people she fired return to thank her for all she did,
because she treated them with compassion and dignity.

We are reminded of lessons from the medical world.[62]
Doctors who apologize for making a treatment mistake
are less likely to be sued. Behaving like a compassionate
human being mitigated the human response of anger and
retaliation, a response that endangered physicians who
made a mistake. People who respond with great compassion
in the face of difficult circumstances are often respected or
even, in some instances, beloved. Why would the act of firing
be any different?

59   Rockwell, D Leadership Freak. leadershipfreak.blog/2012/01/24/letting-people-go-with-transparency-and-dignity/
60   Scott, Kim (2017). Radical Candor. New York: St. Martin's Press. p. 192.
61   Ibid.
62   Medicine is discovering the beneficial effects of compassion on healing as described in Compassionomics: The Revolutionary Scientific Evidence that Caring Makes a Difference, Stephen Trzeciak, MD, MPH and Anthony Mazzarelli, MD, JD, MBE, Studer Group, 2019.

European guidelines for firing employees that apply to larger companies are generally designed to protect the employee's interests, with formally prescribed steps that must be taken to separate an employee from her job. These include well-defined causes and periods of notice. Often, severance payments or Payments In Lieu of Notice are made.

We wish employees were protected in the same ways here in the United States. However, given that we are not, here are some ideas that would have made it easier for the women whose stories are told in this book. Of critical import: when letting someone go, do it in such a way that the people would be comfortable speaking with you at a professional social event, after some initial awkwardness.

BEFORE

- If the company or organization is running out of funds, avoid letting her go by first exhausting other alternatives, such as cutting hours or pay, including those of executives, to preserve the jobs of lower-paid employees. It has to start at the top.

- Ensure that a firing is really necessary and that she is aware that this is a distinct possibility.

- If you are ending the relationship due to performance, make sure you have given the woman a chance to rectify her performance with some kind of progressive performance improvement plan (PIP) that is clearly communicated to her with objective measures of performance. The PIP should not be a surprise to her. You should already have given her some indication that her work was not up to expectations and made clear with what the expectations are. This is simply good management. Give her a reasonable amount of time to make the improvements, at least thirty days, preferably longer. Check in with her during that time to see how it's going and give her guidance. By the end of the PIP, she will know whether she can rise to the requirements of the job, as will you, and the conversation will be almost anti-climactic. Because no employee likes to be put on a PIP, chances are she will already be looking for another job.

- As much as possible, ensure that she has enough time to redress the situation. Don't suddenly decide you have to fire her in the middle of the PIP. If employees know you are going to take the time to help them and address the situation fairly, there will be less fear in the environment.

- Understand that losing one's job is a shock, no matter how prepared you may think she is. Expect anger or tears or both. Don't hold it against her. Be compassionate. Don't let your feelings get in the way. This is *not* about you. You are not the "victim" here—the woman losing her job is. Keep your focus on the right place. Be an emotionally intelligent person.

DURING

- Do it on a weekday (not a Friday) behind closed doors. Consider doing it near the end of the day so she doesn't have to face coworkers if she doesn't want to. Allow the person to save face. Some may prefer to leave at the end of the day; some may need more time.

- Have a box of tissues available.

- Tell her the truth and tell her why you are making this decision in a manner that is not angry or destructive, and that will not leave her feeling ashamed. If you are reading something, have a copy for her to follow along.

- Treat her with warmth: keep treating her as you would any other employee. Let her know she is valued as a person, that she is still part of the "work family" and that you are not breaking those connections that she has built.

- Thank her for everything she did for the organization. Appreciation for her contribution makes a difference in how the person feels toward the organization later.

- Allow her choices: the choice of whether to finish a project or hand it over to someone else. Ask her how much time she needs to put things in order.

- Ask her how she would like to tell people. If you've treated her with dignity, you don't have to be afraid of what she will say to her coworkers. Also, do tell her that after she leaves, you will be telling everyone what happened. Let her help you shape your "joint statement" together.

- Let her have the dignity of cleaning out her own desk, instead of the indignity of someone else pawing through her belongings. She knows what belongs to her, what she wants to keep, and what she wants to discard in your garbage pails.

- Consider whether you have to worry over whether she should have access to the computer system or any other company secrets at this juncture, based on the person herself. Have you gotten indication that she is volatile or vindictive? Then protect your company by shutting off access. But please tell that person you are doing so. Don't let it be a surprise. That activates anger unnecessarily. If she has proven to be trustworthy in the past, make a point of telling her you are continuing her access for a set amount of time so she can finish up projects.

- Leave her phone active; do not turn it off immediately. If you do that, you may leave her stranded with no way to reach anyone for support. What may seem like "business policy" to some is to us unnecessarily cruel. Tell her how long she will have access to the phone, so she can get another one. Or, as one firm does, let her keep the phone and phone number, allowing her to arrange to transfer payment to her own credit card or bank account.

- Let her leave on her own steam. Allow her to say goodbye to people who remain in the office. Please don't have security escort her out of the building as if she were a criminal. If you feel the need for an escort at all, women have felt more comfortable with a boss or colleague seeing them to the elevator.

AFTER

Give the woman a decent severance, one that reflects her contribution to the company, the reality that it will take time to find a job, *and* the fact that unemployment payments are not enough to live on. "Industry standard" is usually woefully inadequate.

- Continue to pay for health insurance for at least three months and up to six months. Yes, there is COBRA, but if someone doesn't have a job, she can't afford to pay her health insurance premiums.

- Don't challenge her unemployment claim. After all, she is not unemployed by her own choice. You made that choice for her.

- Offer to pay for outplacement services for her, either a firm or career coach your company already has a relationship with or a career coach of her own choosing. Caveat: the firm or coach should be able to write her new resume for her. Writing a resume is a specialized task she will not know how to do.

- Call or send an email about a month after the departure to check in on her and offer to be a reference or to pass along her resume to contacts if she wishes. Suggest coffee or a meal. Even though she may not want to talk to you immediately, she may appreciate the thought. This will be most effective in a situation where there has been a downsizing, restructuring, or another no-fault "termination."

- Hold yourself to your highest standards: do not gossip or feed the grapevine. Stick to the story you agreed on with the woman who was fired to maintain an environment of trust and dignity. Ensure that everyone who participated in the termination also upholds the agreement.

PHRASES TO INCLUDE (A SCRIPT)

- Here's what doesn't feel like it's the greatest fit any longer. *(Give examples—none of which should be a surprise to the person after the "Before" section above.)*

- Thank you. We value you and the work you did while you were here. *(Specify so they know you are aware of their efforts.)*

- Here is a severance that represents your contribution to the company, and what we can afford in terms of our budget and precedent (*or in alignment with your severance policy*).

- In a few days, let's write your recommendation together so we can both agree on what to say after you have had a chance to reflect.

- We will give you outplacement services or we will pay for you to have a coach, whichever would be more helpful to you.

- This is a difficult message. How would you like us to handle this information? Would you like to tell your colleagues, would you like us to tell them?

- Why don't you finish what you are working on today or tomorrow and start cleaning out your desk? Let's say that we will close down this position over the next week (two weeks?) so you have a chance to put things in order and we can figure out how to move forward together.

- We value you and we value the work you have done.

We suspect that it is easier for all parties when you treat someone like a human being during the termination process. While still difficult, this kind of termination process at least maintains the human dimension of the professional relationship.

Chapter 31

CONCLUSION

We wrote this book to support women who were fired. And we want to communicate to companies and institutions—to all employers—that the moments when they are letting a woman go can have a dramatic and lifelong impact. More compassion is needed in the process, and women need more support.

Some might say that a compassionate workplace "does not support innovation," that "this is not how business works" or "everything has to move quickly in business to remain competitive." Compassion does not mean that a person is suddenly rendered a wet rag. It means remembering, respecting, and believing in people's fundamental value in every interaction. As you who have picked up this book after being let go may know, as do the brave women who shared their stories with us, it means we can choose to be kind.

We encourage women who have been fired to be kind, first to yourselves, and to extend kindness and good will to those you encounter in the workplace. If you are ever in a position where you have to let someone go, we hope you will do it with the kindness and compassion you wish you had received.

ADDITIONAL HELPFUL RESOURCES

We mention useful resources in the footnotes, so please look at those. Here are additional books, websites, blogs, and podcasts.

Work-Related

MyRightFitJob.com—Tools That Really Work to Find & Do Work You Love. Julia's job search website with practical advice, including scripts. www.myrightfitjob.com.

www.Skloverworkingwisdom.com Blog and source of legal information as well as model memos, letters, and checklists you may wish to purchase. www.Skloverworking wisdom.com.

Hannah Morgan | Job Search, Career and Social Media Strategist for today's job search. careersherpa.net.

Black Women Talk Work podcast, host Myriha Burce. www. blackwomentalkwork.com.

Human Workplace website with podcast, blog, and resources from Liz Ryan, international speaker and HR expert. humanworkplace.com.

Career Tool Belt Alison Doyle's quick, simple advice for every phase of your career. www.careertoolbelt.com.

FairyGodboss, career platform where women empower women. fairygodboss.com.

- Articles include "Five Realities of Being a Latina in Corporate America" fairygodboss.com/articles/5-realities-of-being-a-latina-in-corporate-america and "Five Toxic Thoughts I'm No Longer Tolerating as a Woman of Color in the Workplace" fairygodboss.com/articles/toxic-thoughts-women-of-color-in-the-workplace.

The Corporate Sister, Solange Lopes, CPA, MSA. www.thecorporatesister.com.

Career Advice from The Muse: practical advice on finding a job, exploring career paths, and succeeding in your job. www.themuse.com/advice.

Your Guide to Smarter Job Search—Jobs, Advice, and Resources—Job-Hunt.org, @JobHuntOrg.

"Working at the Intersection: What Black Women are Up Against," Leanin.org. Leanin.org. leanin.org/black-women-racism-discrimination-at-work.

Articles by Dr. Ciera Graham, career coach, writer, and speaker. cieragraham.com/features.

Leadership Freak blog, Dan Rockwell. leadershipfreak.blog.

Websites with employer reviews: Glassdoor.com, Vault.com.

Catalyst.org blog, including Latinx Women's Stories. www.catalyst.org/2020/11/02/latinx-womens-stories.

The Empress Has No Clothes: Conquering Self-Doubt to Embrace Success, Joyce Roché and Alexander Kopelman, Berrett-Koehler Publishers, 2013.

What Do I Do with My Life, Po Bronson. New York: Ballantine Books, 2013 (revised edition).

The Memo: What Women of Color Need to Know to Secure a Seat at the Table, Minda Harts, Hachette Book Group, 2019.

How Women Rise, Sally Helgesen and Marshall Goldsmith, Hachette, 2018.

The Leading Brain, Friederike Fabritius, Hans W. Hagemann. Tarcher Perigee, 2017.

Your Brain at Work, David Rock. Harper Business, 2009.

No Hard Feelings: The Secret Power of Embracing Emotions at Work, Liz Fosslien and Mollie West Duffy. New York: Portfolio/Penguin, 2019.

The Myth of the Nice Girl: Achieving a Career You Love Without Becoming a Person You Hate, Fran Hauser. Mariner Books, 2018.

Advancing Asian Women in the Workplace: What Managers Need to Know, Catalyst, 2003.

Hardball for Women: Winning at the Game of Business, Pat Heim, Tammy Hughes, and Susan K. Golant. Penguin/Random House, 2015.

The Little Black Book of Success: Laws of Leadership for Black Women, Marsha Haygood and Elaine Meryl Brown, One World, 2010.

Personal

Designing Your Life, Bill Burnett and Dave Evans Knopf, 2016.

Women Rowing North: Navigating Life's Currents and Flourishing as We Age, Mary Pipher. New York: Bloomsbury. 2020.

My Grandmother's Hands: Racialized Trauma and the Pathway to Mending Our Hearts and Bodies, Resmaa Menakem, Central Recovery Press, 2017.

In Her Purpose: 40 Principles of Asian Women Redefining Success on Their Own Terms, Rose Buado, Jennifer Redondo-Marquez. In Her Purpose Publishing, 2020.

In Our Prime, How Older Women Are Reinventing the Road Ahead. Susan J. Douglas. New York: WW Norton and Company, 2020.

Your Next Level Life: 7 Rules of Power, Confidence, and Opportunity for Black Women in America, Karen Arrington, The Tiny Press, 2019.

Perfecting Your Pitch, Ronald M. Shapiro with Jeff Barker. New York: Hudson Street Press. 2014.

"The Dangerous Old Woman: Myths and Stories of the Wise Woman Archetype" audio series by Clarissa Pinkola-Estés. www.soundstrue.com/products/the-dangerous-old-woman.

The Confidence Code, Katty Kay and Claire Shipman. New York: Harper Business, 2014.

Good Girls Marry Doctors: South Asian American Daughters on Obedience and Rebellion, Piyali Bhattacharya, Aunt Lute Books, 2016.

I Feel You: The Surprising Power of Extreme Empathy by Cris Beam. New York: Houghton Mifflin Harcourt. 2018.

Post Traumatic Slave Syndrome, Revised Edition: America's Legacy of Enduring Injury and Healing, Dr. Joy DeGruy, Joy DeGruy Publications, 2017.

The Imposter Syndrome Remedy, Dr. Emee Vida Estacio, CreateSpace Independent Publishing, 2018.

When Things Fall Apart: Heart Advice for Difficult Times, Pema Chödrön, Shambhala; twentieth Anniversary Edition, 2016.

ACKNOWLEDGMENTS

Julia: I am so grateful to Suzanne for her steady partnership, wonderful writing and editing, and sense of purpose and humor. She thought we should write about women getting fired and I almost instantly agreed. Thanks to my clients who have taught me what works. Tracey Allard for her generosity in reading a draft, affirming that we two white women got it mostly right, and making great suggestions. John Harvey and Alfred Milanese for running TransitionWorks in Maplewood, NJ. Emily Angell and Alessandra Lusardi at Reedsy who provided early, specific, and useful editing. The Authors Guild for legal advice. My sister Alana and my parents John and Nancy for their encouragement. My friends who knew I was occupied. My writer friends Greg Tobin, Patty Lamiell, and Tommy Nichols for companionship and help. Jill Quist, who helped me find my writer's voice. Joe Cummins for early feedback. Jason Levy, DC, for his enthusiasm. My Smith Chorts for always being there. My coaches Linda Hall, Cameron Hartl, and Elena Pezzini for their support. Jane Kinney-Denning for taking a chance on us, making this book available to women who need it, and hopefully catalyzing a conversation about making work endings less damaging and more compassionate.

Suzanne: I am grateful to many people. First and foremost, to Julia, my wonderful, brilliant coauthor, who I revere. The International Women's Writing Guild (IWWG) encouraged and connected us to Jane Kinney-Denning, who made this book happen. Yaddyra Peralta helped us shape our thinking. My fairy godmother and author, Margaret Winslow, connected us to the IWWG and gave generous feedback. My godfather, Joe Stennett, an adored lifelong presence, offered coffee and cheer, especially (but not only!) when Margie and I talked shop. David Howe shared legal prowess. David Carroll gave helpful advice and connected us to knowledgeable professionals. Colleagues encouraged this project and recognized that this unspoken but common experience of injustice deserved to come to light. Julie knew about Reedsy, where we found Emily Angell and Alessandra Lusardi, who provided early, specific, and helpful commentary. Mary, Geir, and Astrid's formative influences are in these pages. Molly and John are with me always (and Mom and Dad in spirit). Rosemary and Olivia, too. Jenn, Kathleen, and my GFs understood when I just couldn't make it. Antje and The Mid-Century Mods were cool when I took months off from Deutsche Klasse and the band. Jürgen, Faolan, and Artair, and our Ash, I love you.

Julia and Suzanne are grateful to the women who bravely shared their stories, and in so doing became emotional pioneers.

ABOUT THE AUTHORS

Suzanne Vosburg has a PhD in the psychology of creativity and is a writer and photographer (www.suzannevosburg. com). Suzanne's father owned and managed a medium-sized business; he emphasized how important it is to respectfully address conflict and acknowledge emotions for a company to be healthy. He thought this was an essential and often overlooked element in many places of work. In her work in various academic and industry environments, Suzanne has thought a lot about her father's perspective. Her book *Betrayed by Work* pursues her deeply held interest in how people work together.

Julia Erickson is a career and executive coach who helps people find their "right fit" work. A survivor of being fired, she has coached many people who have experienced job loss. Her e-book, *Your Right Fit Job: Guide to Getting Work You Really Love* is available on Amazon and her website, myrightfitjob.com. She has contributed essays to two other books, *A Cup of Cappuccino for the Entrepreneur's Spirit: Women Entrepreneurs' Edition I* and the bestselling *Success from the Heart*. She was Executive Director of two non-profit organizations in New York City over a twelve year period. Prior to that, Julia led public/private workforce development initiatives in NYC government. A graduate of Smith College, Julia has an MBA in Leadership. She was the James Beard Foundation's 2003 Humanitarian of the Year. Julia lives in New Jersey near New York City.

Mango Publishing, established in 2014, publishes an eclectic list of books by diverse authors—both new and established voices—on topics ranging from business, personal growth, women's empowerment, LGBTQ studies, health, and spirituality to history, popular culture, time management, decluttering, lifestyle, mental wellness, aging, and sustainable living. We were recently named 2019 *and* 2020's #1 fastest growing independent publisher by *Publishers Weekly*. Our success is driven by our main goal, which is to publish high quality books that will entertain readers as well as make a positive difference in their lives.

Our readers are our most important resource; we value your input, suggestions, and ideas. We'd love to hear from you—after all, we are publishing books for you!

Please stay in touch with us and follow us at:

Facebook: Mango Publishing

Twitter: @MangoPublishing

Instagram: @MangoPublishing

LinkedIn: Mango Publishing

Pinterest: Mango Publishing

Newsletter: mangopublishinggroup.com/newsletter

Join us on Mango's journey to reinvent publishing, one book at a time.

CPSIA information can be obtained
at www.ICGtesting.com
Printed in the USA
LVHW090755240321
682162LV00001BA/1